The Silence of the Lambs

Yvonne Tasker

 Publishing

For Rachel

First published in 2002 by the
British Film Institute
21 Stephen Street, London W1T 1LN

Copyright © Yvonne Tasker 2002

The British Film Institute promotes greater
understanding and appreciation of,
and access to, film and moving image
culture in the UK.

British Library Cataloguing-in-Publication Data
A catalogue record for this book is available
from the British Library

ISBN 0-85170-871-2

Series design by Andrew Barron &
Collis Clements Associates

Typeset in Italian Garamond and Swiss 721BT
by D R Bungay Associates, Burghfield, Berks

Printed in Great Britain by
The Cromwell Press, Trowbridge, Wiltshire

Contents

Acknowledgments

I would like to thank Rob White who has been an excellent editor
throughout this project, providing invaluable advice and support, and
consistently asking the right questions. Over the years I have discussed
The Silence of the Lambs with many friends, colleagues and students so it is
difficult to single out particular individuals here. However, during the
period of writing Tim Bergfelder, Martin Fradley, Mike Hammond,
Marina Mackay and Sharon Tay have all suggested new directions –
though they may not know it! – and I'm grateful to them. I would also
particularly like to thank Justine Ashby for enlightening discussions on the
gothic, the woman's picture and the possibilities of a feminist cinema.

Finally, I want to thank my partner Rachel Hall to whom this study is
dedicated.

1 Birds, Lambs and Butterflies

Oscar night 1992: host Billy Crystal is wheeled on stage in a Hannibal Lecter-style hockey-mask. *The Silence of the Lambs* goes on to become one of only a few films in recent years to take the 'top' five awards: Best Director for Jonathan Demme, Best Actress for Jodie Foster, Best Actor for Anthony Hopkins, Best Picture for producers Ron Bozman, Edward Saxon and Kenneth Utt, and Best Adapted Screenplay for Ted Tally. Reviewed as a 'chilling psychological thriller' and hyped as the scariest film of the year, *Silence* was only the second R-rated movie to achieve such a sweep, although R-rated films have regularly been awarded Best Picture since the US introduced a ratings system in the 1960s.

The Silence of the Lambs centres on the search for a serial killer, known only as 'Buffalo Bill', who abducts young women seemingly at random: all his victims are white and all are large. Bill imprisons these women in a dry well sunk in the heart of his labyrinthine basement, starving them for three days before shooting and skinning them. Their mutilated corpses are then dumped in rivers across the United States. Finally surfacing in random fashion, Buffalo Bill's victims feed the investigations of an FBI team led by Jack Crawford that has, despite the appearance of five bodies, had little success in tracking the killer. The FBI find themselves literally clueless: the water eliminates trace evidence and no single factor seems to link all the victims to each other or to their killer. Meanwhile, in the privacy of his basement, Buffalo Bill is carefully and skilfully constructing a garment out of the flayed flesh of his victims.

Though Buffalo Bill has been at his work for some time, *The Silence of the Lambs* is tightly structured around the intensive investigation that is triggered by the abduction of Catherine Martin, the daughter of Republican Senator Ruth Martin. Lured into a van – Bill gains her trust by wearing a cast on his arm in the fashion of serial killer Ted Bundy – Catherine is introduced and then abducted about thirty minutes into the movie. From this moment on, both audience and investigators know that they are involved in a race against time. The search for Catherine drives the narrative forward, while the dialogue features repeated references to the passing of time.

The film's premise would already have been familiar to readers of Thomas Harris's best-selling 1998 novel, and in rather more gruesome detail. The novel provides us with details of, for instance, the particular way that bodies decay in water, how they can be scorched in the trunk of a car after death, or the 'fiendishly difficult'[1] aspects of managing human skin, all details that the film sets to one side. Despite his meticulous research – working with the FBI, examining the cases of actual serial killers and so on – Harris is probably best known for creating the rather fantastic character of Hannibal 'The Cannibal' Lecter. In turn, this unlikely role made the well-respected Welsh actor Anthony Hopkins into a fully-fledged film star. A former psychiatrist who killed and ate his victims, Lecter is the film's evil genius, a seductive variety of mad scientist. More importantly in terms of the quest for the killer and for Catherine, Lecter knows the identity of Buffalo Bill.

The FBI, Buffalo Bill and Catherine herself all structure their activities around a three-day cycle at the end of which Catherine will either die or be saved: either the killer or the FBI will have their trophy. While Lecter could reveal what he knows at any time, he has none of the investigators' urgency: 'All good things to those who wait,' he lectures FBI trainee Clarice Starling, and later, as Catherine's time is running out: 'We don't reckon time the same way.' In the scene that immediately precedes Catherine's abduction Lecter demonstrates his knowledge of the killer while hinting at the different sense of time by which he operates: 'I've waited, Clarice. But how long can you and old Jackie boy wait? Our little Billy must already be searching for that next special lady.' Lecter's knowledge allows him to threaten by proxy. Thus, while *The Silence of the Lambs* is in one sense led by the urgent pace of pursuit, it simultaneously follows a different sort of narrative logic, or at least a different narrative *time*, one organised around – and even dictated by – the charismatic Lecter.

Lecter's sense of time is palpably different; both his speech and his movements are careful and measured. Hopkins invests the Doctor with grace as well as malice, both conveyed through small but nonetheless powerful gestures (self-possession evident in the slow closing of the eyes, decisiveness in the movement of a hand, for instance). Lecter spends the

Hannibal Lecter, an observer on display

Catherine Martin held prisoner

majority of the movie imprisoned, his cell a scene to which we repeatedly return. The sense that Lecter is a knowing character is not limited by his restraints or his surroundings – he reaches out from his cell, manipulating others through words and the lure of their own desires. Verbally he is at his most brutal when bound and masked. He induces another inmate to swallow his own tongue with the power of his words – precisely what words might have this power we can only imagine since the act takes place off-screen.

Central to the film's construction in both narrative and thematic terms are four lengthy exchanges between Lecter and psychology graduate-cum-FBI trainee Clarice Starling. Jack Crawford, head of the FBI's Behavioral Science Unit, initiates the first of these meetings, sending Starling to interview Lecter. Her official task is to persuade the killer to complete the Unit's standard questionnaire for the Violent Crime and Apprehension Program (VICAP). Crawford's actual agenda – one he does not trust Starling with as yet – is to engage Lecter with the Buffalo Bill case. Lecter and Starling form an edgy but intense bond. Their exchanges are characterised by the tight facial close-ups that Jonathan Demme and director of photography Tak Fujimoto use throughout, often explicitly aligning us with Starling's point of view. Like Hopkins's performance, these sequences, although they certainly have their chilling moments, are typically still and controlled, something of a contrast to the more frenetic editing we might expect to find in either the thriller or the horror film. Though *The Silence of the Lambs* features some spectacular editing, in these meetings at least it is the use of the close-up that is most visually striking, Lecter and Starling talking intimately through the glass that divides them.

At their first meeting Lecter taunts Starling, almost immediately pinpointing her weakness – an anxiety about appearing common – and playing on it: 'You're not more than one generation from poor white trash, are you, Agent Starling?' Although he dismisses Starling himself, Lecter is disconcerted when another inmate, Miggs, splatters her with semen. Perhaps this excites him, or perhaps he seeks to make amends: either way, telling her that 'discourtesy is unspeakably ugly' to him, Lecter provides Starling with the first of several clues that will involve her ever more closely in the search for Buffalo Bill: 'Look deep within yourself, Clarice

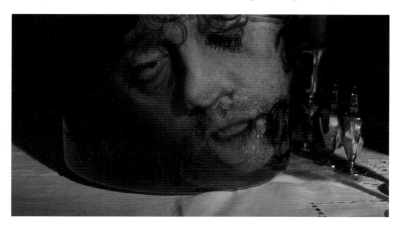

The key to advancement: Benjamin Raspeil's preserved head

Starling,' he tells her. 'Go and seek out Miss Mofet, an old patient of mine.' Following a hunch, Starling visits the 'Your Self' storage facility in Baltimore. Here she explores the contents of a unit rented in the name of Miss Hester Mofet, finding the head of one Benjamin Raspeil (in the process decoding Lecter's anagram: Miss Hester Mofet/miss the rest of me). Raspeil's head is preserved in a specimen jar, an ironic evocation of the laboratories that are so frequently at the centre of crime fictions. This is a laboratory of a rather different kind: inside an old car, the jar is artfully positioned beside a headless mannequin posed with a woman's evening dress and cigarette holder. Though the contents of the car have been undisturbed for years, the sense of purpose that underpins this uncanny scene is as intense as its theatricality.

Returning to the asylum for their second encounter, Starling realises not only that Lecter knows the identity of Raspeil's killer but that she has uncovered another of Buffalo Bill's victims, perhaps even his first. Less formal now and less intimidated perhaps, Starling sits cross-legged on the floor, her hair still wet from the rain. She addresses Lecter directly and frankly. By contrast Lecter remains a mystery, sat at the back of his cell in the darkness. In seductive tones, Lecter makes an offer of assistance in the case and, implicitly, in fulfilling her desires: 'I'll help you catch him, Clarice.' With his riddles, jokes and imperturbable manner, Lecter seems Sphinx-like – his clues are cryptic, the information he provides only ever partial. Yet in pursuit of her quest, Starling must solve the puzzles that Lecter poses.

When a sixth body comes to the surface in West Virginia, Starling is included in the investigation, going with Crawford to examine the body. She spots something in the victim's throat: a bug cocoon. Entomologists at the Smithsonian – first discovered in the darkness playing a bizarre sort of insect chess – identify the pupal stage of the death's head moth. The FBI subsequently discover another such cocoon preserved in Raspeil's head. Here at last, above and beyond the abduction, murder and skinning of women, is the killer's signature. Buffalo Bill wants to transform himself somehow; rejected for gender reassignment he now looks to become not a woman as such, but a sort of human butterfly. Transformation is one of *Silence*'s central themes, and it is typically figured in insect or animal terms: the moth and the bird. The moth or butterfly passes through stages, literally shedding skin to emerge in its new form. The young bird, once dependent, flies the nest when it is fledged, its feathers newly fit for flight.

The imagery of birds, development and flight is most obviously deployed in relation to Starling herself: in the opening sequence, while running in the woods she disturbs a bird which flies off nosily; on their first meeting Lecter tells her to 'fly back to school'. A stuffed owl, wings spread, is the first object found by Starling's torch in the Baltimore storage facility – a little echo of *Psycho* perhaps (the stuffed birds in Norman Bates's back room). The tracking point-of-view shot keeps us with Starling; the stuffed and mounted bird is both a threatening object – a little sign of the uncanny – and a warning of one potential fate, summarised in the contradictory spectacle of a frozen image of movement (though Buffalo Bill wears his victims and Lecter consumes his, both stage bodily transgressions by which they incorporate others). Through the course of the film, we witness Starling pass from trainee to Special Agent (we even glimpse her childhood in two brief flashbacks), a narrative of growth and maturity. Fredericka Bimmel, Buffalo Bill's first

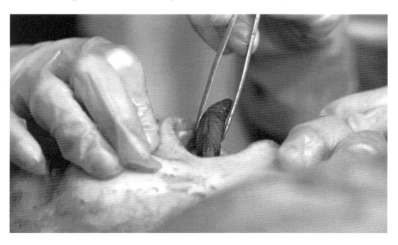

Transformation: investigators discover a moth in the West Virginia victim's throat

victim, is also associated with birds. Photos on her bedroom wall show happy scenes with her father at the pigeon coop, the background embellished with childish drawings of birds and branches. Lecter also describes Buffalo Bill through the analogy of the bird, casting Raspeil's murder as 'a fledgeling killer's first effort at transformation'. Beyond her name, Catherine Martin has little of the bird about her, although this much links her to Starling.

Other than the obvious – he escapes capture – transformation is not at issue with Hannibal Lecter. He remains seemingly fixed throughout. If any animalistic metaphor were to suggest itself, it would be reptilian (though in Harris's novel he strikes Starling as a 'cemetery mink' who 'lives down in a ribcage in the dry leaves of a heart'[2]). Lecter typically mocks and even exploits the labels that are assigned to him (whether to induce fear or to lull others into a false sense of security). In their third interview, Starling attempts to take the upper hand. Brushing aside the self-important asylum director Dr Frederick Chilton, she puts a false offer to Lecter in Senator Martin's name (thus explicitly usurping a powerful woman's authority). In return for his help, Lecter will be transferred to another institution. Starling masks the FBI's false offer with a perverse detail given the film's use of animal imagery – the island where he will have a week's freedom each year is an animal disease research centre. Lecter agrees to help but only in return for personal information from Starling: she promises Lecter a beach with nesting terns, but he quickly insists on turns of a different kind: 'I tell you things. You tell me things. Not about this case though: about yourself.' In this way, Lecter's suggestion that Starling look deep within herself takes on a darker significance. Probing at pain, Lecter asks for Starling's worst memory of childhood; she gives him the death of her father, a town marshal shot when interrupting a burglary. Orphaned at ten years old, Starling was sent to a sheep and horse ranch in Montana, running away after only a few months. Once he has got into her memories, Lecter openly admits a fascination with Starling: 'I think it would be quite something to know you in private life.' The film seems to invite us to share this fascination, so that we contemplate Starling even as we are positioned with her.

In return for her secrets we learn, with Starling, of Buffalo Bill's investment in transformation, that he believes himself to be a transsexual but that he is not – yet again, another label is required. We hear Lecter's final words of warning about Buffalo Bill's terrible pathology over an image of a tape recorder; Dr Chilton is listening in on Starling's imposture. Bent on career aspirations of his own, Chiltern reveals the deception and brokers an actual deal with Senator Martin. The stage is set for Lecter to finally leave his cell: camera and editing combine to suggest that escape is foremost in the Doctor's mind. In a hangar at Memphis International Airport, the heavily restrained Lecter is wheeled out to meet Senator Martin. This exchange is quite different in character from those between Lecter and Starling. Though graceful in his cell, the restrained Lecter is all malice. Attention focuses on his eyes and what little we can see of a mouth behind the distorting mask. Lecter gloats over the Senator's pain in this sequence, revealing a little of his brutality. Providing a false name, Louis Friend (another anagram Starling unravels – iron sulfide/fool's gold – not that anyone cares to listen), Lecter is to be rewarded with a change of scenery. In the meantime he is held in an improvised jail in Memphis. It is here that the fourth and final exchange with Starling takes place.

Lecter's point of view

In their final encounter, power has definitely shifted, with Lecter taking the upper hand once more: 'People will say we're in love,' he mockingly suggests. Indeed, Starling has no official reason to be there – she must sneak in under false pretences now: quite a contrast to the almost cocky manner she adopted in their third meeting. While she dismissed Chilton on her way to make the false offer, at the end of this meeting she will herself be forcibly removed from the scene. Having 'no more vacations to sell', Starling must reveal the secret behind her sudden childhood departure from the sheep and horse ranch. It is this story that introduces the film's third source of animal imagery – the lambs of the title. Waking one night to the screaming of the spring lambs being slaughtered, the young Clarice attempts to free them. When the lambs will not move, she runs away, taking one with her. She fails to get far however: ultimately she is sent away from the ranch and her lamb is killed. In contrast to birds and moths, lambs have little to do with transformation – they are slaughtered and eaten as young rather than adult animals (to the young Clarice their screams sounded 'like a child's voice'). Moreover, lambs don't have the sense to save themselves. In telling this story Starling is at her most vulnerable: even as she recalls the stubborn refusal of the lambs to run away, Starling seems to lose herself in her recollections, almost as if she were hypnotised by Lecter's voice and fixed to the spot.

In *Silence* it is sacrifice rather than transformation that the lamb suggests. For Starling, speculates Lecter, Catherine takes the place of the lamb; the quest to save Catherine is thus also a personal search for resolution. The lamb does not have the opportunity to reach maturity, to transform into a different, adult being but 'poor Catherine' (as Lecter terms her) might yet be saved. Perhaps lambs stand in for all victims, just as Foster's Starling signifies heroism both in a generalised and a specific sense. Of course Starling herself is also associated with the lamb and thence with sacrifice – Lecter sketches her as a classical figure, holding her lamb in her arms as though it were a child. Publicity shots also exploited this image with at least two different poses of Starling/Foster with a lamb. In this way an image that appears in the film only through Lecter's sketch is transformed into a narrative image of a different kind: both maternal

Jodie Foster poses rather uncomfortably with a lamb …

… while Starling is idealised in Lecter's drawing

and, by association, Christian, Starling and the lamb invoke ideas of sacrifice and of innocence. For his last meal in captivity Lecter demands 'lamb chops, extra rare', as if he wished to devour Starling by association. The arrival of the meal provides him with his opportunity for escape; in the aftermath, the red of the meat and of human blood once more links death with consumption.

From this point on, *The Silence of the Lambs* becomes a rather different sort of film: Lecter escapes from under the noses of the police, while Starling sets off, a renegade now, to track Buffalo Bill. Lecter's escape is violent – perhaps the goriest spectacle the film has to offer. Appropriate perhaps, since we are now moving towards horror more explicitly. Following a final clue left by Lecter in her case-file, Starling returns to the first of Buffalo Bill's female victims, to the source of it all. Her method is to get inside the victims' lives, visiting the Bimmel home, talking to her friend Stacy, following up on her sewing work. During

Starling's investigation of Fredericka Bimmel's domestic surroundings she comes to understand what Buffalo Bill is doing, sees the craft and skill he is investing in the creation of a woman-suit. Although the FBI already have a name, Starling is left to follow up leads and connections. Finally and unexpectedly, Starling finds herself confronting the killer in his lair, shooting him dead and saving Catherine. In the coda, we see that Starling has achieved her goal, passing out as an FBI Special Agent. She shakes Crawford by the hand; he tells her that her father would have been proud (a moment that is the film's only wrong note as far as Amy Taubin is concerned[3]). In the midst of the celebrations Lecter phones Starling for a last conversation and to reassure her that she is safe, from him at least. The film's punchline – 'I'm having an old friend for dinner' as Chilton steps off a plane – reassures *us*, as it were, that Lecter has not changed his ways. *Silence*'s grimly comedic final image is of the dapper Lecter disappearing into the crowds in pursuit of his former jailer.

Setting out to write this book, ten years on from the initial release of *The Silence of the Lambs*, Lecter was in the news once more. A cinematic follow-up to *The Silence of the Lambs* had been a possibility – almost a certainty, Harris permitting – since the critical and commercial success of Jonathan Demme's film. Rumours over casting kept the idea in the news while Harris wrote at his own pace. At one point Anthony Hopkins was reported to be reluctant to reprise his role for fear of encouraging violence. Harris's long-awaited fourth novel, the third to feature Lecter, was finally published in 1999. *Hannibal* was an instant – and distinctly weird – best-seller which ends with Starling and Lecter forming a perverse outlaw couple. Jodie Foster equivocated over the script, ultimately refusing to reprise her role as Clarice Starling. While the search for her replacement may not have quite matched that for Scarlett O'Hara, actresses from Gillian Anderson to Gwyneth Paltrow were linked with the role, maintaining the publicity until Julianne Moore was cast in the part shortly before filming commenced. The DVD release of both *The Silence of the Lambs* and *Hannibal* in 2001 was accompanied by rumours of a new adaptation of *Red Dragon*, the first Harris novel to feature Lecter, which had been filmed by Michael Mann as *Manhunter* back in 1986. Such a move would not be surprising since, while the figure of Lecter commands immense public interest, the endings of Harris's and Ridley Scott's *Hannibal* are so completely divergent that it becomes difficult to imagine an adaptation of any further instalment the writer might produce.[4]

In some ways, *Hannibal* the book was more of a phenomenon than *Hannibal* the film. The same could not be said of *The Silence of the Lambs*, although the book certainly was high-profile, a best-seller that was also critically well-received. Detective fiction has long been considered the most respectable end of genre fiction and Harris invested the thriller with a psychological and narrative complexity that turned on the heroic role of the FBI's Behavioral Science Unit. In turn, Demme's film introduced Harris's work to an even wider reading public, laying the ground for *Hannibal*'s subsequent success.

Working with film, I'm a little wary of drawing comparisons with prose fiction. The two media employ different techniques for narrating, or for that matter, terrifying. It is hardly a surprise that cinema is typified by an intense investment in the visual, or that words might figure differently in fiction and in film. Nonetheless, talk of adaptation often seems to take place in an abstract, hierarchical mode – a hierarchy in which literature seems to emerge as almost by default 'better', more complex than film. Gavin Smith offers a rare reversal of the hierarchy in relation to *Silence*, arguing that what he terms the 'film's reinvention' of Harris's novel 'is in some way more potent because the genre is *essentially cinematic*, its central device the voyeuristic-subjective camera'.[5] Fiction and film each involve us in a different relationship to vision. With thrillers and horror narratives, vision turns as much on what is suggested as what is 'seen', the spectacle of violence in particular. Perhaps this is why popular discourse on the cinema returns again and again to the question of how *much* we see – many reviewers sought to reassure viewers of *The Silence of the Lambs* that they would 'see' little; others protested that the film showed us too much.

The danger of cultural prejudice aside, it would be a mistake to sideline Harris's *The Silence of the Lambs* in pursuit of Demme's film, not least since it is such a remarkable book. Certainly the film aims to be a faithful adaptation; both performers and members of the production team make repeated references to Harris's novel in interviews. There are plenty of minor differences between novel and film. But the key difference is one of tone – of all the narrative voices in *The Silence of the Lambs*, Harris's is the most powerful, subtly spinning the presentation of his characters' thoughts. While Demme's *The Silence of the Lambs* sets the grim modernity of Quantico and serial killer gothic off against each other, both are in turn contrasted to the everyday world of the victims: the scenes around the Bimmel home in Belvedere, Ohio, or the West Virginia funeral home are poignant, filled with the drab little touches that bring these spaces to life. In this, Demme's film is more compassionate, and more self-consciously liberal than Harris's book. Harris constantly comments on the action, the settings and the desires of his characters. As Starling realises how transparent she seems to be to Lecter's gaze (*'He sees very clearly – he damn sure sees through me'*), Harris notes: 'It's hard to accept that someone can understand you without wishing you well.'[6] Though Lecter's malicious mind games are the obvious referent here, Harris could just as well be commenting on the ambivalence of his own prose.

Starling investigates Frederika Bimmel's girlish world

Consider the scene in which Starling visits Fredericka Bimmel's home. Both Harris and Demme show us a 'shabby neighborhood' on a sunny winter's day. The incidents described are more or less similar: Starling tries to find a feel for the dead girl's life, discovers items linked to sewing and realises that Buffalo Bill is skilled in dress-making. Yet the tone of novel and film is subtly different. 'Fredericka did not display photographs of herself in the room,' Harris tells us, presumably since (like Bill, it is implied) she is not content with her body or herself: Fredericka's room betrays 'an echo of desperation'.[7] In this bleak space, Starling becomes acutely aware of her own physicality (and implicitly her superiority): 'Starling saw herself in the full-length mirror on the end wall and was glad to be different from Fredericka.'[8]

The film by contrast immerses Starling in Fredericka's world, a little pathetic in the traces of friendship and affection perhaps, but girlish rather than desperate. Starling's eyes, signalled through the camerawork, pick out a series of photographs: four showing Fredericka with her father at the pigeon coop (in the last a bird is released); Fredericka with her cat and best friend Stacy; baby photos in tiny frames. Finally, Starling turns to the music box, finding hidden photographs of Fredericka, a secret stash seemingly overlooked by other eyes. The screenplay incorporates details

Starling pursues Buffalo Bill into his basement world

from another scene in the novel here, one in which Starling visits
Catherine Martin's apartment and finds explicit photographs of the
Senator's daughter 'coupling'[9] with an unidentified man. The film's
polaroids show Fredericka posing flirtatiously, and rather childishly, in her
white, outsize underwear; seen so long after her gruesome death, these
secret images seem naïve rather than saucy. Harris makes the point with
rather more cruelty: Fredericka's letters to Gumb are discovered at his
home after his death. Starling can hardly bring herself to read them,
'because of the hope in them, because of the dreadful need in them'.[10]

For Harris, Fredericka is a character who does not display herself
but who is laid bare nonetheless; for the film she is captured in a visual
image, indeed multiple images of her smiling face which suggest that her
life was not only about failure. Harris leaves little unexplored. The net
result is both a greater sense of understanding of the novel's multiple
characters and, ironically, a heightened sense of cruelty, an awareness of
the danger that any sort of desire brings. Crucially, Ted Tally's screenplay
focuses our attention on Starling and her relationship with Lecter,
eliminating the novel's multiple subplots concerning, for example, the
illness and death of Crawford's beloved wife, Bella. This streamlining
process continued through to the final cut with scenes featuring Crawford
in particular trimmed back. The film also explicitly offers Starling's point
of view, aligning the audience with her heroic quest. The tracking point-of-
view shot, more usually associated with danger in thriller or horror films,
provides us with Clarice's perspective, both in the flashbacks to her
childhood and the here and now of the investigation. Extreme close-ups in
which characters talk direct to camera add intensity to the exchange of
looks and words. Harris's vision is bleak, at times undercutting Starling's
heroism. By contrast, Demme's film enacts a heroic quest narrative in
which the heroine's motivation is clear and direct. The film does not
simply allow Clarice Starling her autonomy; it is positively celebrated.

2 The Sum and the Parts: Horror, Crime and the Woman's Picture

The opening sequence of *The Silence of the Lambs* centres us firmly with Clarice Starling. Pounding through a Quantico assault course at daybreak, exertion is evident in her sweat and the sounds of her breathing. We grasp her determination and strength at the same time as we sense her vulnerability, a generic suggestion of threat implicit in the image of a young woman running through the woods alone: mist rising, a disturbed bird flying off, the evocative orchestral score underpinned by the sounds of insect life. Both mobile camera and fragmented editing suggest narrative questions: is someone watching, is she being chased? The answer is both yes, and no. While Starling is neither watched nor chased here, the questions prepare us for the drama to follow. She will become the object of Lecter's scrutiny and, although she spends most of the film in pursuit of Buffalo Bill, ultimately she will – albeit briefly – take up the position of the hunted. At a more symbolic level, Starling is in flight from her past and during the course of the narrative she must come to terms with painful memories.

Although the movie begins with images of Starling alone, she has significant relationships: with the two serial killers, Lecter and Buffalo Bill; with the somewhat stern Jack Crawford; with her long-dead father; with fellow trainee Ardelia Mapp and, crucially, with Buffalo Bill's female victims whom she seeks to avenge and protect. Thus, although she is marked as something of a loner in this opening sequence, Clarice Starling is positioned at the centre of a network of characters and institutions, the seemingly fragile connection that ties them together.

Genres as well as characters connect complexly in this film. The type of movie we take *The Silence of the Lambs* to be depends a lot on which particular connections we choose to pursue. A hybrid creation, *Silence* grafts together elements from horror, the woman's film and the police (well, FBI) procedural. Each of these genres involves distinctive ways of rendering the ideas about reason, madness, gender, sexuality and identity that make up the film's thematic terrain. Victim and seeker, Starling appears in different generic guises within each.

Whether Starling is a renegade for an age in which the PI no longer seems to be viable, or the androgynous, embattled figure that Carol Clover dubs the 'final girl' of the slasher film, *The Silence of the Lambs* is a rarity in contemporary American cinema – a rites of passage narrative centred on a female protagonist. It is also very much a woman's picture, in both that

Starling tackles the Quantico assault course

Visually singled out, Starling is a small figure in a male world

Starling investigates the Your Self storage facility

genre's gothic and contemporary manifestations. At its most basic the
woman's picture can be defined as a film with a female protagonist, dealing
with issues related to women and women's lives, and ultimately privileging
a woman's point of view. Ted Tally's screenplay focuses squarely on
Starling, while Demme consistently foregrounds female point of view.
Interviewed at the time of *Silence*'s release, Demme emphasised the film's
place within the cinematic inheritance of the woman's picture: 'Ever since
my days of working with Roger Corman, and perhaps before that, I've been
a sucker for a woman's picture. A film with a woman protagonist at the
forefront. A woman in jeopardy. A woman on a mission. These are themes
that have tremendous appeal to me as a moviegoer and also as a director.'[11]

The woman's films of the 1940s were organised around a clash, and
typically a choice, between the protagonist's career, or perhaps her
independence, and the possibilities of romance. More recently the
woman's film has shied away from this conflict, centring firmly on either
female friendship or romance, with work and career appearing as little
more than a backdrop.[12] For Jeanine Basinger,[13] the classical woman's
picture has little to do with setting or with genre as it is often understood –
the noirish *Gilda* (US, Charles Vidor, 1946) and the pirate-romp *Anne of
the Indies* (US, Jacques Tourneur, 1951) can equally be termed women's
pictures within her definition. The woman's film, that is, should not be
simply mapped onto either melodrama or the domestic. Yet in almost all
its versions, the woman's picture involves romance, something that *The
Silence of the Lambs* seems to deliberately lay to one side. In a genre where
women's danger is repeatedly signalled in sexualised fashion, *The Silence
of the Lambs* rigorously avoids eroticised violence. Instead we follow
Starling's struggle to establish her identity, to come to terms with her past
as she transforms herself. This restraint is all the more surprising given that
the film centres on Buffalo Bill's search for an identity through the bodies
of young women.

Among the studies in perverse and heroic masculinities to which it
has been compared – *Seven* (US, David Fincher, 1995), say, or *Manhunter*
– only *The Silence of the Lambs* fully mobilises the, to me, compelling
figure of the female investigator. Her particular rite of passage begins with

her as a trainee dispatched by Crawford on an 'interesting errand', and ends with her triumphing over Buffalo Bill and rescuing Catherine Martin. In turn Starling's journey is framed against the killer's perverse attempts at transformation. But it is Starling/Foster's spectacular brand of ordinariness that the film showcases – poor but stunning, gifted but inexperienced, she struggles both to understand a killer's mind and to resist being marginalised within the institutions of law enforcement. Excess (hysteria, even) is pointedly left to the film's male psychopaths. B. Ruby Rich describes Jodie Foster's star persona precisely in terms of the 'extraordinary ordinary – a hyperrealism of character that mixes class traits and gender attributes into a singular but vulnerable strength'.[14] These qualities are well-suited to Foster's role in *The Silence of the Lambs*: we encounter Clarice Starling within both scenes of mundane, everyday experience and of the most fantastic adventure.

Does the film's focus on the female investigator render it transgressive somehow? Perhaps, although not in the obvious way; whatever the term might mean, *The Silence of the Lambs* is not in any straightforward way a feminist film (consider the articulation of femininity as perverse ambition in relation to Buffalo Bill, for instance). Quizzed on this issue, Demme was equivocal: 'I did like that *The Silence of the Lambs* was a woman's picture. Is that vaguely subversive? – I don't know.'[15] Nonetheless, the film reinvigorated the cinematic career of a character type already firmly established as a figure of fascination in popular literature – the female investigator. A skilled and sometimes even a powerful figure within the institutions of law enforcement, the female investigator comes up against obstacles different from those faced by her male counterparts. The most fundamental of these is that she must perpetually convince others of her abilities and/or her legitimacy just as Starling struggles to do. Despite the best-selling exploits of heroines from Paretsky's V. I. Warshawski to Cornwell's Kay Scarpetta or, more recently, Kathy Reichs' Dr Temperance Brennan, in cinematic terms the role of Starling is exceptional. In the ten years since its release, Foster's role has attracted as much interest as the charismatic Lecter. Yet in the same period virtually no other high-profile mainstream movie has featured a female

investigator who operates alone as Starling does.[16] The previous year's
Blue Steel (Kathryn Bigelow), in which Jamie Lee Curtis appears as a
rookie cop in pursuit of a serial killer who happens to be her boyfriend,
similarly seemed to presage a figure whose cinematic career was never
quite fully realised.

There are plenty of movies with female investigators (both
professional and amateur) in partnerships, and many of these show the
influence of *The Silence of the Lambs*: Holly Hunter and Sigourney Weaver
in *Copycat* (US, Jon Amiel, 1995) for instance, Denzel Washington and
Angelina Jolie in *The Bone Collector* (US, Phillip Noyce, 1999) or Mulder
and Scully in television's *The X-Files* (which piloted in 1993).[17] The DVD
cover for *The Cell* (US, Tarsem Singh, 2000) quotes a *Vogue* review:
'Jennifer Lopez sizzles in a *Silence of the Lambs* style psychological thriller'.
Nearly ten years on the serial killer has become, it seems, an acceptable
subject for a summer release: *The Cell*'s tagline 'This summer ... enter the
mind of a serial killer' underlines the point.[18] There are certainly
similarities between *Silence* and *The Cell*, where the labyrinth of the killer's
mind provides the gothic equivalent of the old dark house. Yet the *mise en
scène* is thoroughly eroticised, while the first section of the film elaborates
the killer's ritualistic necrophilia. Moreover, though Lopez's child
psychologist, Catherine Deane, enters the alien space of the killer's mind
alone, she is soon entranced by his eroticised world and needs cop Vince
Vaughn to rouse her. One of the most widely reproduced images used in
marketing the film pictured Deane/Lopez tranformed into a sort of siren.

British television's *Prime Suspect*, scripted by Lynda La Plante and
first broadcast in 1991, provides a very different reference point for
Silence. Featuring Helen Mirren as tough Detective Chief Inspector Jane
Tennison, the first instalment centred on the hunt for a sadistic serial killer,
played by John Bowe as a mild-mannered figure (the ability to disappear
into the everyday precisely characterises the idea of the serial killer as the
stranger in our midst). *Prime Suspect* netted Mirren a Best Actress BAFTA
(the British equivalent of an Oscar), and several sequels followed –
television is, after all, a serial medium in the way that the cinema once was.
Jane Tennison is a figure of authority, heavily invested in the patriarchal

institutions of law enforcement within which she struggles to succeed, in a way that Starling is not.

Despite such small-screen successes, the cinema seems reluctant to let the investigative female protagonist work alone. Thus, if *The Silence of the Lambs* makes mainstream use of exploitation success, as Carol Clover[19] suggests, it also draws heavily on other sources, crime fiction in particular. In turn, the repertoire on which the film drew and which it also helped to establish has thrived in fiction and on television. Orion, the company that produced *Silence* (and which went bankrupt prior to its Oscar sweep), had scored a hit in the 1980s with the long-running, female-oriented crime show, *Cagney and Lacey*. Perhaps it is not surprising then that for those American reviewers of *The Silence of the Lambs* who emphasised Starling's

Investigating women: Weaver and Hunter in *Copycat*

The Cell: The killers fantasy world transforms psychologist Catherine Deane (Jennifer Lopez) into a femme fatale

investigative role, it was not the cinema but Nancy Drew – upper-class, girl adventurer heroine of popular fiction and, latterly, television – who provided a reference point.[20]

Of the films that followed, *Copycat* most closely resembles *The Silence of the Lambs*. The two female protagonists, Holly Hunter's cool San Francisco cop and Sigourney Weaver's agoraphobic criminal psychologist play victim/investigators to Peter Foley's copycat serial killer (he reconstructs the crimes of previous killers, staging crime scenes to match frozen images from the past). Others such as *Seven*, *Kiss the Girls* (US, Gary Fleder, 1997) and the follow-up, *Along Came a Spider* (US, Lee Tamahori, 2001), *The Bone Collector*, and *The Cell*, all follow in this developing tradition. In each case, the drama revolves around a potent mix of horror and psychology with the killer's identity pursued through what is in effect an elaborate puzzle.

As a high-profile *horror* movie, the success of *The Silence of the Lambs* signalled a shift by which the genre moved into the mainstream of US cinema during the 1990s. If the film and the marketing campaign that promoted it reached for prestige as well as thrills, the possibilities of exploitation were always present. Of the film's lurid subject matter, Daniel O'Brien wryly suggests that '[e]ven Roger Corman … would probably draw the line here'.[21] Jonathan Demme had of course got his first chance to direct through Corman's New World operation (debuting in 1974 with a women in prison movie, *Caged Heat*) while Corman himself appears briefly in *Silence* as FBI director, Hayden Burke. Both the huge commercial success of Demme's film and its credibility with mainstream critics subtly redefined the popular cinema, suggesting the viability of a mass audience for adult horror. Clearly *The Silence of the Lambs* is mainstream horror in a quite different way to the teen-oriented, parodic movies more usually associated with the 1990s (Wes Craven's *Scream* [US, 1996] or *I Know What You Did Last Summer* [US, Jim Gillespie, 1997] for instance). If the film broke new ground in terms of the mainstream, as I would suggest that it did, it was through its distinctive generic combination and its pitch of horror to an adult rather than a teenage audience.

When Harris's *Hannibal* was released to high expectations in 1999, it was as a pre-sold property, quickly adapted for the screen with Ridley

Scott as director. The adaptation of *The Silence of the Lambs* was not so straightforward. Although the commercial failure of the previous Harris adaptation, *Manhunter*, was doubtless a factor, the difficulty of bringing *Silence* to the screen places us squarely with the question of taste. At the actor's instigation, Orion had optioned the book for Gene Hackman to direct and possibly to star in, but Hackman was ultimately put off by the violence. Surprising as it may seem from today's perspective, he was not alone. O'Brien cites a studio executive's distaste: 'Nobody wants to see a movie about skinning women.'[22] Similarly Michelle Pfeiffer, Demme's first choice for the role of Starling, declined since in the director's words 'the material proved too strong for her'.[23] Jodie Foster pursued the role vigorously. Foster had recently taken a Best Actress Academy Award for her performance as Sarah Tobias, the tough survivor of a gang-rape in *The Accused* (US, Jonathan Kaplan, 1988). Ironically she too would withdraw from the sequel, saying of the Starling character: 'I would never betray a person to whom I owe so much.'[24]

The focus on psychology and psychopathology which typifies *The Silence of the Lambs* – profiler as dark hero; psychiatrist as anti-hero; serial killer as sexual misfit – is a characteristic of what we now think of as upmarket horror film and fiction. Indeed, Carol Clover has lamented what she sees as the up-scaling of the slasher film represented by movies like *The Silence of the Lambs*, films which 'come awfully close to being slasher films for yuppies – well-made, well-acted, and well-conceived versions of the familiar story of a female victim-hero'.[25] For critics like Clover it is precisely the film's respectability that counts against it – *Silence* is somehow too middle-brow (and decidedly 'low-risk'[26]). Richard Dyer also contrasts *Seven* to what he terms the 'strained affirmation'[27] found in *Silence*. It is certainly not my purpose here to argue that Demme's film is somehow really much grittier or more culturally marginal than has been hitherto supposed. The film has no aspirations to the experimental. It resolutely resists the bleak, urban atmosphere characteristic of so many psychological thrillers in search of kudos. Nonetheless, for director Jonathan Demme, the 'big concern was to avoid the typical great shadowy thriller look because stories like this in which the lonely law enforcement

Unseen, Buffalo Bill
watches Catherine
Martin through infrared
goggles

Lieutenant Boyle
grotesquely transfigured

person is tracking the terrifying killer can overuse effects like long
shadows. I really didn't want to employ the traditional prose of the thriller,
which I was trying to get away from.'[28] Though the film self-consciously
defies our generic expectations, as Gavin Smith writes: 'There's nothing
hip about *Silence*.'[29]

Silence's horror lies in both characters – Lecter, Bill – and scenarios,
the display of violence and more particularly its aftermath. In horror
terms, Lecter is a plain, that is to say charming, figure of evil. The film's
very premise – Buffalo Bill's ghastly scheme – is horrific. 'Whatever else he
may be,' writes Clover, 'Bill is the clear brother of Norman Bates,
Leatherface, Jason, Mark (of *Peeping Tom*), and the rest: a male who is a
physical adult but a spiritual child, locked in the embrace of his mother.'[30]

William Blake, *The Great Red Dragon and the Woman Clothed in Sun* (c. 1806–9, Brooklyn Museum, New York)

Hieronymus Bosch, *Christ Carrying the Cross* (c. 1490, Musée des Beaux Arts, Ghent)

And Starling's trajectory is very much in line with Clover's formulation of the final girl as victim-hero. The suggestion of horror in the opening sequence is matched by Starling's basement confrontation with Bill/Gumb, as he stalks her in the darkness with the assistance of the infrared goggles with which he had earlier spied on Catherine. Here, for the first time, the film abandons Starling's point of view: instead we see her through the killer's eyes, flailing around in the darkness. Both Bill's basement and the asylum in which Lecter is held are unmistakably gothic, though the look of the film as a whole is much more everyday, even naturalistic at times. Emphasising as it does the small signs and clues that make up the painstaking process of collecting evidence, such everyday detail – in the scenes around the Bimmel home for example, or the funeral home in West Virginia – is more in line with the police procedural than the horror film.

By contrast, the violence of Lecter's attack on Lieutenant Boyle and Sergeant Pembry evokes the slasher, as does the grotesquely theatrical staging of their deaths, the sheer extremity of the crime scene that Lecter leaves in his wake. The brief scene in the ambulance, the punchline of the escape in which Lecter peels off Pembry's bloody face to reveal his own, equally red, lips parted in a seeming smile, is also a slasher moment: we see the threat before the hapless victim in a dramatic two-shot. This is arty slasher though: Boyle is transfigured into an angel, fixed to the bars of Lecter's former prison, his body opened up for our inspection. Another winged creature, Boyle's carefully arranged body is echoed in the scene that features Buffalo Bill (wearing somebody else's hair as Lecter will wear another's face in making his escape) presenting himself to the camera; when he raises the colourful wrap around him he is transformed into a butterfly of sorts. If Boyle is turned into an angel or a butterfly, Lecter's tableau is also a grotesque sort of crucifixion. Indeed, *Silence* exploits a tradition of dark, religious iconography that extends from Hieronymous Bosch through William Blake (a key figure for Harris) to Francis Bacon, Kristi Zea's immediate inspiration for the grotesque crime scene.[31]

In a film of suspenseful editing and close-ups, this is one of the few scenes from which the camera pulls back rather than closes in (the other most striking instances all centre on Starling: a tracking point-of-view shot as she is led away from Lecter's Memphis cell; the camera pulling back from a close-up of Gumb's gun on the stove out of her sight and, finally, from her shocked face as she repeats Lecter's name into the phone). Glimpsed first through the frosted glass door panes, then seen through the reaction shots of the Memphis police and an extreme close-up, Boyle's body is artfully presented by both Lecter and Demme. Perhaps the camera movement is also something of a clue, suggesting that we might usefully look elsewhere. Boyle's spectacular corpse dominates the scene, shifting attention from the body on the floor – the body that we assume to be Pembry but which is actually Lecter wearing not only the Sergeant's uniform but his face. As this may suggest, the crime scene in *The Silence of the Lambs* represents a puzzle to be decoded as much as a site of horror.

While horror has recourse to evil and the supernatural, the detective narrative centres on interpretation, and leads towards explanation. In this sense, the different ways in which the film treats its two serial killers is, in part at least, dictated by generic conventions. True, Buffalo Bill is a monstrous figure, but he remains explicable: there is nothing of the supernatural about him as there is with the uncanny figure of Lecter. The discovery and analysis of clues and of physical evidence structure the investigative narrative. In *Silence*, think of the discovery of Raspeil's head, the examination of the victim's body in West Virginia, the crime scene photographs and trips to the Smithsonian: all fit the investigative mould. Yet the equal, if not greater, importance given to psychological evidence – profiling the killer, understanding or even intuiting motivation – suggests a slightly different focus, one very much associated with Harris and the contemporary thriller.

The Silence of the Lambs is not only relatively talky; it is also a film that has been much talked about. Much of this talk has centred on the politics of representation (is Buffalo Bill gay, whether implicitly or explicitly?; is Clarice a role model?) and on the ethics of imagining violence (is Lecter too appealing for our own good?). And it seems clear that these images mattered to critics partly because *Silence* was in so many ways a prestige picture, a medium-budget endeavour with known and respected stars that was potentially slumming it, moving into the territory of exploitation. In classical Hollywood, studios thought of certain projects as prestige pictures. Such movies were often adapted from a well-regarded source, whether Shakespeare, Tennyson or a best-selling novel such as Margaret Mitchell's *Gone With the Wind* (not typically, we might note, from horror or crime fiction). As Tino Balio writes, the prestige picture was 'not a genre'. Instead, the term related to 'production values and promotion treatment'.[32] *The Silence of the Lambs* was only medium-budget in contemporary terms (with its $22 million budget, it was certainly no *Cleopatra*), yet the analogy is nonetheless useful. A high-profile adaptation, characterised by narrative and thematic complexity, *Silence* benefited from an advertising campaign that promised horror and psychology in equal measure. Aiming for an adult, middle-class audience not typically associated with the horror genre, to some extent at least, *The Silence of the Lambs* can be understood as a contemporary prestige picture.

Promoted as a thoughtful genre piece

Of course, the fact that *The Silence of the Lambs* was seen to have cultural significance has much to do with its huge commercial success. The film set box-office records, grossing over $130 million dollars. For obvious reasons perhaps, unsuccessful films are rarely read as symptomatic in the way that *Silence* was at the time of its release. Predictably, and despite all the praise that the film received, reservations tended to centre on the question of just how much distance there was between *Silence* and more obviously exploitative horror fare. A few immediately disdained the film as exploitation cinema for the middle-classes. Yet *The Silence of the Lambs* was broadly welcomed by critics, who praised the film's serious tone and literate approach to the subject of serial killing, as well as the careful construction of suspense and the quality of the performances. Some months before sweeping the board at the 1992 Academy Awards, *Silence* had a major success at the New York Film Critics Circle Awards winning Best Film, Best Director, Best Actor and Best Actress. Other awards such as the Silver Bear at the Berlin Film Festival served to underscore the strength of *Silence*'s central performances as well as its reputation as a complex genre piece.

Mark Seltzer has identified a 'peculiar mixture of moral and feral intentions' in 'the media fascination with serial murder'.[33] Certainly *Silence*'s success triggered both fascination with the charismatic Lecter (and with cannibalism in general) and something approaching dread as to the film's potential effects. The question in relation to *Silence* became one of tone – what kind of message was the film sending? Its success was framed by

Silence as up-market slasher

two other scandalous serial killer texts, Bret Easton Ellis's novel, *American Psycho,* and the long-delayed release of the edgy, low-budget *Henry, Portrait of a Serial Killer* (US, John McNaughton, 1986). Critics found *Silence* to be disturbing primarily on two counts: an association embodied by Buffalo Bill 'between homosexuality and pathology, between perversion and death'[34] and, conversely, a sense that the film celebrated Lecter despite his violence, a celebration regarded as both morally troubling and rather snobbish (since Lecter is so explicitly coded as 'cultured' against Buffalo Bill's inarticulate white trash). Some praised *The Silence of the Lambs* for its rendition of a complex, autonomous female protagonist – *Village Voice* critic Amy Taubin proved a particularly cogent and powerful defender[35] – while others found the characterisation of Starling troubling. Thus, while *Silence* was widely read as symptomatic, critics disagreed as to precisely *what* it was symptomatic of.

Accusations of homophobia may not have hurt *Silence*'s box-office, but they did have a significant effect in generating debates concerning sexuality and representation. A few weeks into the film's US release, the *Village Voice*, in a piece perhaps rather ambitiously subtitled 'Sorting Out the Sexual Politics of a Controversial Film', invited comment from a diverse group of writers. Amy Taubin and Martha Gever both responded scathingly to a review (by Ron Rosenbaum in *Mademoiselle*), which had declared *The Silence of the Lambs* to be harmful to women. By contrast, Larry Kramer and Stephen Harvey both suggested that the film would do untold damage to gay men, whether in terms of their self-esteem or in terms of attacks from others. 'Should this movie incite some credulous homophobe out there in the dark to work out his problem in the streets, Lecter and Gumb won't be the only ones with blood on their hands,' wrote Harvey.[36] At a time of queer activism fuelled by anger at state inaction over HIV and AIDS, the moment that also generated what B. Ruby Rich would term new queer cinema, criticism of *The Silence of the Lambs* was fairly traditional: a call for, more or less, positive images. In any case, it was the film's very status as a well-regarded genre picture that provided a hook for a high-profile and angry campaign around sexuality and mainstream representation.

It makes no sense to simply set aside people's pain, to say that those male gay critics who found *Silence* homophobic were somehow wrong. Nonetheless I see little evidence that gay men saw themselves in Buffalo Bill – rather the fear was that *others* might see gay male sexuality in that image of deviance. Not recognition but misrecognition was at issue in relation to *Silence* then, a dynamic we might contrast to the following year's *Basic Instinct* (US, Paul Verhoeven, 1992). Although controversial (and, indeed, effectively protested by lesbian and gay activists) for its murderous bisexual heroine, the film nonetheless attracted enthusiastic support from at least some lesbian viewers.[37]

Though there are other markers of his deviance – the swastikas in his basement, for instance – Bill's perversity is certainly bound up with gender. His misogyny – he treats women as objects, preferring to address Catherine only indirectly as 'it' – is that of the wider world writ large. Since sexual identity – identity in general – is such an important part of the film, it is no surprise that this aspect has attracted so much attention. For many critics, Demme's film lacked the complexity of Harris's novel in accounting for Buffalo Bill – instead the film was felt to fall back on images of gender deviance and of gay male identity as psychopathic yet effeminate. Crucially, this is a question of vision, of the intricacy of words versus the supposed simplicity of images. Harris's meticulous prose is set against the horror film's accretion of visual signs and gestures (nipple ring, poodle, 'swishing'). The film's diverse but striking imagery polarised critics; gay men and feminists, both typically intensely critical of mainstream images, found themselves at odds over the meaning of *The Silence of the Lambs*, reading it in very different ways. Moreover, critics found themselves at odds in a very personal and very intense way. Committed liberal Jonathan Demme no longer seems to speak about *The Silence of the Lambs* publicly – both his and Foster's voices are notably absent from the lengthy documentary included in the Special Edition DVD.

While debate tended to focus primarily on sexuality, it is in many ways gender that provides the key to the difficult politics of a movie like *The Silence of the Lambs*. While we may respond to Starling's development of traditionally masculine virtues, the film nonetheless employs grotesque imagery connected with both the female body (the very concept of Gumb's woman-suit, but also the visceral aftermath of the abandoned bodies) and femininity in the form of Buffalo Bill himself.

Analysing the debates surrounding the film over the first few months of its release in the US, Janet Staiger found female critics unanimously supportive of the movie and of Foster/Starling's role in it. In the years that have followed, the film has received a lot of attention from feminist writers, as well as from those interested in representations of gender and sexuality and the horror film. From the perspective of some feminists, the controversy surrounding the film's sexual politics was effectively (and unfairly) displaced onto Jodie Foster in a telling conflation of the performer's personal silence around her sexuality and the film's supposed sexual dishonesty. In this interpretation, a strong woman is liable to end up (like the lamb, so to speak) sacrificed. As Staiger notes, the preoccupation seemed to be with Foster and not with Starling, the star image rather than the character or performance. The effect was to render a heroic figure into a victimised one. For B. Ruby Rich: 'The campaign turned [Foster's] life and career into a sinister prize in a new contest of so-called "outing" that

Jame Gumb transfigured for the camera and an audience of mannequins

Gumb's woman suit

In the climatic basement confrontation, Gumb reaches out towards Starling

seemed more intent on gathering this private woman's skin for a trophy than even Buffalo Bill had been.'[38] A desire to peel away the image to find the truth that lies underneath is, of course, a central component not only of star discourse but of ideas about sexual identity. The attempt to 'out' Foster represents an alternative, extra-cinematic effort to get under the skin, to fix her (to fix any) identity.

If gay men had good cause to object to Buffalo Bill's 'swishing', feminist critics, well-used to picking over images of women in mainstream cinema, certainly had cause to feel resentment at the way in which responses to *Silence* simply ignored both its female protagonist and its female victims. Feelings were no less fraught almost a year later when the film was winning awards. Responding to Jodie Foster's speech at the New York Film Critics Circle Awards, one writer sneeringly dismissed her perspective on the character she plays in precisely these oppositional terms: 'so it's feminism one, gay pride zero'.[39] Not all critics were even convinced that Starling was so 'positive' for feminism. Brian Jarvis, for example, tells us that while at 'a glance' *The Silence of the Lambs* 'might appear to be promising territory' for a 'progressive representation of the feminine', the film is ultimately a disappointment: 'Agent Starling's autonomy is continually compromised as each of her major decisions are seen to be determined by her relations with male authority figures.' 'Clarice' (like Lecter, critics – myself included – cannot seem to resist using her first name at moments when we think we know what's going on inside), he continues, 'joins the FBI to follow in the footsteps of her dear dead papa.'[40] Case closed. But then we might recall that Clarice Starling does not simply follow but exceeds her father – only ever a town marshal – in her career. 'Is that a good job, FBI Agent? Get to travel around and stuff, I mean better places than this?' bored Stacy Hubka asks her in a Belvedere drug store. In one sense Starling has gotten away, though critics still did their best to bind her to daddy.

3 Detection and Deduction

'BILL SKINS FIFTH': the banner headline of *The National Inquisitor* on the wall of Jack Crawford's office provides the audience with its first glimpse of Buffalo Bill, visualised through his crimes. The surrounding crime scene photographs also provide Clarice Starling's first introduction to the victims. In fact we see these images through her eyes, as it were – her casual curiosity as she casts around Crawford's office turns to a look of troubled concentration, shock registers in her face and in the arms that fall to her side. As the camera moves in, allowing us to briefly scan polaroids of partially flayed bodies, the sombre orchestral music re-emerges. The dead staring eyes of female victims are juxtaposed with their smiling faces in portrait-style head-shots. The 'BILL SKINS FIFTH' banner, together with the single word 'TERROR!', clipped from a newspaper, appears again in Gumb's basement. After Starling has shot the killer dead, the camera zooms in to pick up this detail, suggesting closure of a sort. Such a visual link is no coincidence – both the FBI and the killers that they seek keep their clippings. At a deeper level, *The Silence of the Lambs* offers a parallel of sorts between the official FBI investigation of the dead body and Gumb's precision in flaying his victims. Killers and detectives, that is, are all skilled at their work, although they have different ways of getting under the skin.

Jack Crawford assigns Clarice Starling an interesting errand

Physical evidence is at the core of the investigative fiction: the business of documenting and analysing fingerprints, tyre tracks, weapons and other objects, images and bodies. In recent years, the intensely specialised analysis of physical evidence has become a familiar feature of crime narratives. Similarly crime fictions, which once showed cops struggling with computers, now use information technologies as a standard part of the plot. Developments such as DNA testing have helped to oust the PI in favour of a specialised kind of police procedural, one requiring access to specialist information, as Joyce Carol Oates[41] points out. Indeed, increasingly elaborate descriptions of the analysis of weapons (saws, knives, bullets), body parts (bone, teeth, flesh) and body fluids (blood, semen, saliva), not to mention fibres and fingerprints, form an important part of contemporary crime fiction. The pathologist has become an investigative hero (and one who is typically much more high-tech than television's *Quincy*), while the autopsy has become a grim set piece of film and television series. The television show, *CSI: Crime Scene Investigation* (CBS, 2000–) with its relish of scientific techniques, the painstaking analysis of physical evidence alongside intuitive investigative work, is a case in point.

In contrast to the intricate forensic techniques of crime fiction, *The Silence of the Lambs* seems positively low-tech: we never see Starling at a computer terminal, for instance, or even in a laboratory. The post-mortem examination of the West Virginia victim is the key scene to foreground physical evidence. This is the only occasion when we see one of Gumb's victims in the flesh, and it functions as one of the film's most memorable sequences. We've seen that *Silence* eschews the noirish aesthetic of despair that *Seven* would later employ to the hilt. 'Let's make this film bright … let's allow the audience to see everything,'[42] Demme recalls telling Tak Fujimoto. Here, seeing everything is less about gore and more about contemplating the aftermath of Bill's crimes. The body of the woman (whom Lecter will later scathingly refer to as 'Miss West Virginia') is mottled and muddy; leaves and other debris from the river cling to her, while her flesh has an unpleasant sheen, whether from the water or from decay is unclear. Where her flesh has been removed, we see the fat and tissue that lie beneath the shell of the skin.

Starling preserves the evidence

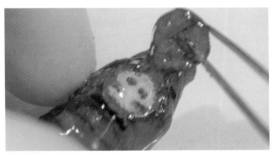

Detection and detail: entomologists identify the death's head moth

The examination of the victim's body is a generic but nonetheless a powerful image. Obviously such scenes confront us with matters of mortality, specifically with a life cut short. The corpse – she is never named – is both repellent and pitiful. In a grotesque sort of naturalism, we see the details of physical deterioration and violence – in the hand and broken fingernails, for instance (later we'll see, with Catherine, bloody marks and broken nails embedded in the wall of the well where the dead woman was once imprisoned before her). Reaction shots of Crawford and local officials emphasise the intense smell of the decomposing body – the sight of the FBI men smearing ointment under their nostrils prepares us for this. Starling's response is less direct, reflected as it is in the glass doors of a cabinet. When she turns to view the body, she whispers one word, 'Bill'. Forensics and the details of physical evidence, even the elaborate workings of psychology, are the territory of detective fiction and the police procedural, but the examination of the corpse marks a territory shared with horror. Though it may well be true, as Barbara Creed writes, that '[t]he ultimate in abjection is the corpse',[43] it is hard to see the West Virginia victim as simply an image of abjection, perhaps because the ability to preserve humanity while remaining dispassionate enough to analyse the details of death, is so explicitly at stake here.

It is Starling, whose voice wavers as she begins to examine the body, who mediates an emotional response that goes beyond disgust. Her role as investigator involves the intensity of empathy, though the display of forensic knowledge places her in a rather different relationship to the victims whose bodies and lives she interrogates. What relationship does she establish with the female victims and with the woman she hopes to save? The fact that this body surfaces in West Virginia is no coincidence: the location serves as a reminder of Starling's origins, suggesting a possible link between the two women so apparently different. Starling can read the signs, is able to spot straight away that this is the body of a woman who

The West Virginia victim

Clinical detail observed with empathy

even in death does not quite belong: 'she's not local – her ears are pierced three times and there's glitter nail polish: looks like town to me'. Ironically, it is the woman she saves that Starling least resembles – Catherine Martin's affluent, big blonde as against her slim brunette who struggles for recognition; Starling's status as orphan contrasts sharply with Catherine's powerful and influential mother.

Though Demme's *The Silence of the Lambs* was more often discussed in the same breath as Easton Ellis's *American Psycho*, its release also followed fast on the publication of Patricia Cornwell's *Postmortem* in 1990. The first of her highly successful series of novels featuring Richmond-based Chief Medical Examiner Kay Scarpetta, *Postmortem* quickly gathered both acclaim and sales. The search for a serial killer centres on the slab, as Scarpetta reconstructs the shape of the crime and the identity of the killer through meticulously detailed attention to the victim's body and to the crime scene. Bodies are picked over for minute traces of the crime, the analytic processes employed intricately described at every stage. In Cornwell's fiction the autopsy and forensic analysis take centre stage.

The autopsy is also a staple, if not a cliché, of the television series *The X-Files* (featuring large in an episode in which the series parodied its own conventions) as FBI agent Dana Scully (Gillian Anderson) meticulously cuts up bodies and dispassionately diagnoses natural and unnatural causes of death. Cool and crisp, Professor Sam Ryan (Amanda Burton) also works the crime scene and the body in the upmarket British crime drama, *Silent Witness* (BBC, 1996–). It seems there is something potent in this juxtaposition of professional women and corpses, this rather perverse manifestation of the caring professions with which female characters have so long been associated.

The post-mortem examination of the body is a central scene for *The Silence of the Lambs* in both a thematic and narrative sense. The discovery of the moth provides an insight into Buffalo Bill's ritual. But the sequence is also a turning point in another sense, representing Starling's inclusion in the investigation – recall that she has been officially invited to participate, although she remains a trainee. In case we miss the point, the process of exclusion and then recognition is played out for us in miniature. As

Crawford, Special Agent Ray Terry and Starling arrive, they encounter resistance from the local police. Crawford steers a frosty Sheriff Perkins away, hinting that this kind of sexual violence should not be discussed in front of a woman. Starling is left isolated in an anteroom, surrounded by curious cops: as the camera pans, once more giving us her point of view, they stare blankly out from the screen. Amidst the chaotic scene that follows, the local police clutching their Styrofoam cups as they stand, chatting obliviously, around the body bag that contains Bill's latest victim, Starling finally asserts herself; politely but firmly she instructs the men to leave. The body and the clues it can provide are, it seems, her provenance.

The feature that Starling and Cornwell's Scarpetta most obviously share is their distinctive combination of professional detachment and intense personal involvement. Blood and gore, injuries carefully and objectively recorded on the one hand; emotion, a powerful empathy with the (typically female) victims of violence on the other. Both women are investigators, albeit of different kinds, who have channelled their ambitions into careers within suspicious, male-dominated institutions. An obvious difference between the two lies in Scarpetta's position and institutional power as against Starling's youth, marginality and inexperience. Yet in *Postmortem*, Scarpetta finds herself uncomfortably identifying with the victim of the killing with which the novel opens, a young surgical resident. Moreover, memories of the isolation experienced during her years of study (she is a qualified lawyer as well as a medical doctor) are triggered by her treatment at the hands of male politicians and

Chilton confronts
Starling

cops: 'survival was my only hope, success my only revenge', she recalls.[44] If the PI has been replaced by the FBI and the CSI, the investigator as heroic outsider remains a staple of the genre: a figure vulnerable enough for us to feel that she (or he) is imperilled, just as she is human enough for us to find our way into the austere institutions and complex bodies of knowledge that crime fictions mobilise. Both Scarpetta and Starling are constantly challenged; though they are figures of authority in one sense, they must also struggle for respect. In this world, knowledge and professional achievement are necessary weapons. And, as we'll see, the mobilisation of such themes within *The Silence of the Lambs* is part and parcel of its debt to the woman's film.

While medical detail produces a dispassionate approach to the decaying human body, mutilation recorded in clinical terms, Starling's initially shaken voice and observations on the victim as an individual (her ear piercings, her glitter nail polish) indicate compassionate rather than dispassionate interest. Indeed, a literal, empirical description is insufficient for the job of catching the killer. Lecter invites Starling to look *beyond* the physical evidence to the motive behind Gumb's actions. It is not until she has taken this step that she can confront the killer. In *Silence* it is not the crime, or even the 'scene of the crime', but the reconstruction of its stages and, crucially, the attempt to establish *motive* that is played out. The principal crime scene that we 'see' enacted is Lecter's – and not Bill's – in the shape of the orchestrated carnage that he leaves to mask his escape. The *mise en scène* of horror, whether in Crawford's office, Lecter's cell(s) or Bill's basement, retain a status not simply as spectacle but as puzzles for the audience to decode should we wish.

The moth cocoons, one found stuffed into the West Virginia victim's throat, another discovered in Raspeil's carefully preserved head, represent a piece of physical evidence – opened with precision, the death's head moth is identified immediately by the entomologists (the process takes rather longer in the novel). Yet the evidence only reveals its significance within an empathetic narrative, that is, Bill's desire to become something else and the moth's function as symbol of this. Speculating on the origins of the specimen, one of the entomologists observes: 'somebody grew this guy; fed him honey and nightshade, kept him warm. Somebody loved him.' Lecter continues the thought, telling Starling: 'The significance of the moth is change: caterpillar into chrysalis or pupa, and thence into beauty.' As in archaeology, objects become evidence through both physical analysis (carbon dating, chemical analysis) and acts of speculation and interpretation. It is not only the profiler who offers psychological testimony, or who shows a capacity for insight.

In its delicate balance of physical evidence and speculative interpretation, *The Silence of the Lambs* is of course quite in keeping with crime fiction where the play of reason and deduction (Holmes or Dupin, say) is frequently partnered by intuition. Moreover, crime fiction is seldom reluctant to confront us with the spectacle of death. Both reason and violent spectacle are present in Poe, for instance: the rationalising of Dupin and the excess of gothic horror. 'The Murders in the Rue Morgue' features both the excessively *'outré'*[45] nature of the crime itself (involving mutilation and extreme violence committed by an escaped orang-utan) and the careful processes of reasoning by which the investigator arrives at his conclusions.

Towards the climax of *The Silence of the Lambs*, the full force of the FBI, its high-tech plane flying blindly in the wrong direction, is juxtaposed with Starling's slow progress, amassing interviews in Belvedere, Ohio, as she follows up on Fredericka Bimmel's small-town life. 'We wouldn't have found him without you: nobody's going to forget that, least of all me,' Crawford tells Starling before cutting her off – she is left repeating his name to a dial-tone, prefiguring the end of the movie when Lecter makes his surprise phone call from Haiti.

These disparate images of the FBI at work – low-tech footwork and high-tech assault – are knitted together in a sequence of spectacular parallel editing that deliberately deceives the audience. Having identified Buffalo Bill as Jame Gumb, Crawford and his heavily armed team make their way to Calumet City, preparing to storm into Gumb's house. Meanwhile in the basement, latest victim Catherine Martin and Gumb are engaged in a stand-off: Catherine has enticed Gumb's dog, Precious, into the well, demanding a phone. Infuriated, Gumb goes for his gun, pacing the basement and shouting: forced to address Catherine as a person for a second time, he bellows to her with menace – 'You don't know what pain is.' At this moment of confrontation the doorbell rings. Cross-cutting generates suspense as we are led to expect an armed confrontation. Instead when Gumb finally opens

Crawford and his team prepare to besiege an empty house …

… while Starling happens upon Buffalo Bill during routine enquiries

the door it is to the diminutive figure of Starling. In the follow-up, the FBI team storm into an empty house (in the thriller at least, guns a-blazing does not necessarily signal narrative closure). As the camera closes in on Crawford's face he realises Starling's danger, whispering her name – 'Clarice' (that intimate form again). In a sudden reversal, Starling is no longer marginal, finding herself instead at the centre of the action. This sequence nicely dramatises the sense that Starling both is and is not – or not yet, at any rate – part of the organisation ('not real FBI' as Lecter puts it). Moreover, it sets up the woman-in-peril sequence in the basement that follows – the part of the film that most explicitly invokes horror.

Though we may move firmly back into horror in this climatic confrontation, *The Silence of the Lambs* holds us throughout with its measured narrative of detection and deduction. Starling begins by picking her way through Lecter's anagrams: Miss Hester Mofet/miss the rest of me; when Lecter names Louis Friend as the killer, only Starling doubts him. Lecter identifies Gumb's chief desire – he covets – asking Starling to understand this in terms of her own life, her experience as coveted object. In going to Belvedere, Starling follows up on the Doctor's hint that Gumb may have known his first victim Fredericka Bimmel ('we covet what we see every day'). From the dress-making dummy in the Bimmel home she deduces the nature of Gumb's endeavour (the wallpaper's faded butterfly motif, glimpsed only briefly, provides another small clue). Both the moth as a symbol and dress-making as a sinister means to an end come together once more in the brief, charged moment when Starling realises she is standing in Gumb's house. Looking round the room as Gumb asks her about the progress of the investigation, her eyes pick out a moth landing on spools of colourful thread. Turning to face her, Gumb asks at precisely this moment, 'You got like a description, fingerprints, anything like that?' But it is not such evidence that has led Starling to him. The message is clear. Although it comes down to a fight in the dark, catching the killer lies in understanding. Starling has to learn about vision: to see and to understand the smallest signs.

Empathy can be used in very different ways, however; it has different cadences. In *Manhunter*, Will Graham's capacity for empathy is typically bound up with judgment finding expression in the form of an accusation. Graham feels his way into the killer's fantasy, reconstructing his movements and inner thoughts. Gazing up close at the monitor that replays home movie footage of a slaughtered family, Graham addresses the absent killer: 'You took off your gloves to touch her, didn't you? Didn't you, you son of a bitch?' His insight into the killer's fantasies leads to a partial print, lifted from the eyes and nails of his victims.

Starling empathises not with Buffalo Bill but with his victims. She gets inside their lives. In Harris's novel it is clear that Starling's empathy is somewhat edgy in relation to the privileged Catherine Martin. Her feelings are for the big, lower-class women who have been stripped of even their bodies that did not quite fit: 'It was Kimberly that haunted her now. Fat, dead Kimberly who had her ears pierced trying to look pretty and saved to have her legs waxed. Kimberly with her hair gone. Kimberly her sister. Starling did not think Catherine Baker Martin would have much time for Kimberly. Now they were sisters under the skin.'[46] Harris's malicious coda punctuates Starling's involvement in the case in a way that the film refutes. In the film, Starling's empathy is victim-centred and, above all, compassionate. By contrast, Lecter's immense capacity for an understanding of desire and experience is consistently used to malicious ends. Lecter's observations cause Starling pain in their very first encounter ('You see a lot, Doctor,' she concedes: he goes on to lead Miggs to his death through words). His comments to Senator Ruth Martin, sneered from behind a distorting mask, are even more disconcerting than those to

Manhunter: Profiler Will Graham's (William Peterson) capacity for understanding allows him to track the killer

Starling, exploiting the mother's fear for her child. After asking if she had breast-fed Catherine, Lecter coldly observes: 'Amputate a man's leg and he can still feel it tickling; tell me, ma'am, when your little girl is on the slab, where will it tickle you?'

Given the centrality of psychological probing to the narrative of *The Silence of the Lambs*, and the construction of profiling as almost mystic within FBI fictions more generally, the interest of Lecter is not simply that he is a simultaneously attractive and repellent figure. After all, isn't the psychiatrist already a figure we love to hate, or at least despise? Lecter delights as he confirms our worst fears in an off-hand remark on the murder of a former patient: 'Best thing for him really. His therapy was going nowhere.' Characterised as fraudulent in so many movies, the analyst nonetheless fascinates, holding out the promise of self-knowledge. For Harvey Greenberg, *Silence* seems preferable to the other big analysis movie of 1991, Barbra Streisand's *The Prince of Tides*. Of Lecter he notes: 'one sees him exorcize Clarice Starling's childhood trauma of paternal loss, emblematized by her identification with the slaughtered lambs, with surprising empathy, if in just a few behind-bars sessions'.[47] Yet the moment when Lecter thanks Starling for her story, indeed the whole process of

Lecter as monstrous therapist – invasive and knowing

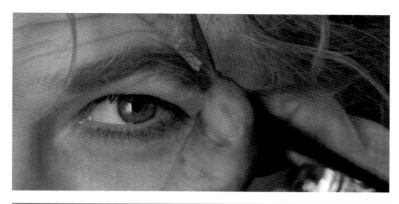

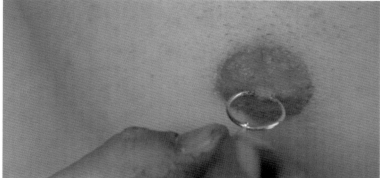

Yearning for transformation: Gumb's investment in femininity as display

probing itself, suggest a malicious pleasure in the pain of others, in uncovering the memories that have been so carefully hidden.

Although she sees through Lecter's act to some extent, Starling struggles to understand Gumb's motivation. She realises after seeing the dress-maker's dummy and fabric cut to pattern in the Bimmel home that Gumb knows how to sew, that the patches of skin he has taken from his victims are pieces of an intricate pattern for the woman-suit he is constructing. Yet she never really expresses any desire to understand *why* Gumb does what he does, to get inside his head in other words. Ironic perhaps, since the film contrasts a dark analogy between the two, both figures yearning for transformation. Only Lecter offers any kind of explanation for Gumb's crimes, speaking – albeit briefly – of the killer's failure to understand his own identity: 'Billy is not a real transsexual, but he thinks he is; he tries to be. He's tried to be lots of things I expect.' Lecter also touches on questions of the origins of violence – nature or nurture – suggesting that Buffalo Bill experienced a traumatic childhood: 'Our Billy wasn't born a criminal, Clarice, he was made one through years of systematic abuse.' As Seltzer notes, 'Child abuse – wounded as a child, wounding as an adult – is one of the foundational scripts in accounting for the serial killer.'[48] In the absence of further words, as an audience we are left largely with images – and the monster of horror – on which to base our profile. Not insignificant perhaps, given the controversy that was to surround the film's presentation of Buffalo Bill as a perversely feminised killer.

The FBI is not typically imagined in empathetic terms. Indeed, the

The profiler: criminal psychologist Helen Hunt in *Copycat*

more common image of the Bureau is rather more uptight; rule-bound rather than improvisational. Smartly dressed, impassive, college-educated, decidedly middle-class and decidedly male, the FBI agent of the movies is quite different to the typical cinematic cop (who is much more likely to be blue collar). In both *Red Dragon* and *The Silence of the Lambs*, Harris has recourse to a rather different version of the FBI, one centred on the Behavioral Science Unit and the figure of the profiler. Harris's sources for Crawford, Robert Ressler and John Douglas (the latter would act as a consultant on the film), have both published accounts of their work. Thus, as Seltzer notes, the image of the profiler has a popular currency in true crime literature as much as crime fiction. To some extent the two draw on each other: 'The mindhunter works by simulation too. He works – like Poe's prototype detective, Dupin (one of the crime-fiction sources Douglas cites) – by identifying himself with the killer.'[49] Like Fox Mulder's spookiness, the profiler and his/her strategies of imagination and identification mark something of a break from the traditional image of the FBI.

Cornwell's Scarpetta sees the profiler as magical, almost as supernatural-seeming as the phenomena – serial killers – that they investigate: 'Profilers are academicians, thinkers, analysts. Sometimes I think they are magicians.'[50] As a cinematic and literary phenomenon the profiler is a great success (setting aside the 'real' world for now). Though not a profiler as such, *Seven*'s Detective Somerset (Morgan Freeman) also exemplifies the type. He is, as Dyer notes, 'the site of wisdom in the film'; 'the importance he attaches to the clues and his interpretation are correct. In narrative terms, he is the one who knows.'[51] Such immense wisdom is obviously something of a fantasy, but a compelling one, particularly in a narrative context that sets out to explore the unknown and the dreadful. Seltzer charges *The Silence of the Lambs*, both novel and film, with offering an 'adulatory representation'[52] of the FBI profiler. Yet profiler Crawford emerges as a forbidding figure in Demme's film, while Starling is a seeker of a much more complex type. Harris is also less romantic than Seltzer supposes: 'Crawford,' he tells us, 'ever wary of desire, knew how badly he wanted to be wise.'[53] The desire for wisdom is as much a fantasy as Buffalo Bill's desire for transformation; each is a goal that can only ever be partially achieved.

4 The Female Gothic

For all its commitment to psychological profiling and forensic evidence, *The Silence of the Lambs* leans to the gothic. No surprise perhaps since the modern murder narrative and the gothic novel are more or less contemporaries. Karen Halttunen shows how, towards the end of the eighteenth century, preachers' sermons that had presented the murderer as simply one sinner among a community of sinners were gradually replaced by more lurid popular accounts centred on the brutal details of the crime itself. Along with 'the rapid growth of the cult of horror'[54] that she intricately maps came the construction of the murderer as 'moral alien'[55] rather than ordinary citizen. The murderer is now exceptional rather than mundane, cast like the villain of the gothic novel as monstrous in character. Although the serial killer may be a more modern phenomenon, he too may be cast in gothic terms, even as psychology attempts to construct an explanatory framework for his crimes.

There is a clear opposition in *The Silence of the Lambs* between modern and gothic spaces. The cold concrete of Quantico was envisaged by Demme, Fujimoto and production designer, Kristi Zea, as 'clinical, kind of lifeless'. Lecter's cell by contrast was conceived in terms of the 'emotional potential of the more gothic kind of look'.[56] Gothic geography is by definition disorienting and disturbing – haunted castles, old dark houses and tormented landscapes are its archetypal spaces. Gothic buildings are sinister even when domestic: attics, basements and forbidden chambers house secrets and threaten danger. Such sites, fantastic manifestations of the mind, are echoed in *Silence*'s claustrophobic evocation of Lecter's asylum cell, an archaic place visited by investigators seeking to somehow capture the essence of the serial killer. Starling must walk the gauntlet to reach Lecter; beyond his cell, which is the farthest from the security of the watching guards and orderlies, we glimpse another staircase. Though we never learn where this leads, there is perhaps a suggestion that the labyrinthine space of the asylum extends yet further.

Buffalo Bill's basement (of the rest of the house, we see only the hallway and a disorderly kitchen) is equally spatially complex. A series of

The asylum basement

rooms centres around the well that holds Catherine prisoner. Equipped with numerous knives, home to moths in various stages of development and peopled with mannequins, the basement represents an elaboration of Bill's fantasies of which the woman-suit is simply the most extreme manifestation. As if this world might become pervasive, we encounter an uncanny use of mannequins throughout *The Silence of the Lambs*. In the scene arranged with care in the Baltimore storage facility, Raspeil's preserved head is mocked by a mannequin's body. Yet more mannequins discreetly preside over the foyer of the Memphis courthouse where Lecter is held, silent witnesses to the SWAT team's confusion. The dress-maker's dummy in the Bimmel home and the mannequins in Bill's basement, not to mention the partially completed woman-suit itself, contribute to this sinister iconography of disembodied and dehumanised personhood.

Just as she will later enter Buffalo Bill's basement, Starling's journey to Lecter's cell takes her insistently downwards. Her first approach to Lecter in the asylum is a compelling sequence. A combination of mobile camera, rapid editing and a dizzying shot down a stairwell takes us from Chilton's office, through an outer office, three corridors and yet more steps. Our movement through these transitional spaces is disorienting. It also evokes the inescapable sense of a journey, or more accurately a quest, commencing. Starling must pass through no fewer than five barred metal doors in order to reach Lecter. At the third, bathed in red light, Chilton pauses. In an obvious challenge to Starling's nerve, Chilton confronts her with a photograph of the damage Lecter inflicted on a female nurse when she was tending to him. Horror is both promised and withheld here – we do not see the picture, only Starling's face shot from below as she views it. Here, at the end of the descent – they have come as far down as they can go – Starling suggests that she confront Lecter alone (we see the disgruntled Chilton leave on a security monitor). The stage for Starling's first meeting with Lecter is thus elaborately set. When we finally meet him, the killer's careful manner and calm speech are something of a contrast to the rather lurid suggestion of violence that went before. Lecter is a monster of a special sort: in the terms of the gothic we are charged to be wary of his words as well as his actions.

Though *Silence*'s emotional intensity stems most obviously from its use of close-ups, the design of the production is absolutely central to its effect as horror. The film employs a resolutely muted palette. Browns, greys and blues dominate, with occasional glimpses of green (Starling's slightly childlike duffle coat or her embroidered sweater, for instance).

Lecter's violence revealed and concealed

'You keep to the right': asylum orderly Barney acts as gatekeeper

Both Quantico and the world of the film's two serial killers are typically bland in colour – only occasionally enlivened by red shirts at Quantico, or the fabrics, jewellery and thread in Buffalo Bill's home. Catherine Martin's lurid blouse is discarded at the scene of her abduction in favour of a grey jump suit. Gumb reserves colour for himself, most spectacularly in the scene that has him performing his fantasy identity for the camera, first swathed in a wrap, then raising his arms like a butterfly's wings.

Michael Mann's colour-saturated *Manhunter* seemed to deliberately eschew both the gothic and the everyday. The protagonists inhabit a world that is stylised even when it is presenting ordinary life: the scenes between Will Graham and his son in the supermarket, say, or the blue light that pervades Graham and Molly's home by the sea. Lecter's cell, located within a high modernist facility, seems bleached out: white uniform, white walls and bars. As Lecter, Brian Cox seems to merge with his surroundings, an effect that serves to emphasise his face. Appropriate, perhaps, since Lecter's words and even his thoughts are as dangerous as his teeth. *The Silence of the Lambs* alludes to this look in the Memphis prison scenes where Lecter is dressed in a similar uniform of white vest and trousers. Lit from above, Hopkins leans forward so that while his face remains in shadow, his body is bathed in light. In extreme close-up it is almost as though the head has been set free from the body. Holmes we may recall once said, 'I am a brain, Watson. The rest of me is a mere appendix.'[57]

If the bare stone of Lecter's Baltimore asylum cell suggests a dungeon, in Memphis Lecter is contained and even displayed very differently. The cage that acts as a sort of temporary cell is positioned at the centre of a large room. Privileges restored, Lecter's cell is furnished with a screen, an antique table and rug. Music and books are now at his disposal; the cell has the faux-domesticity that we might expect of a therapist's office (and which also characterises Crawford's office with its makeshift bed and homey lamp in the corner). Though Lecter is well-lit, the corners of the room are dark; we can discern paintings on the wall but little detail. Before he leaves, Lecter will rearrange the red, white and blue bunting that surrounds the hall, using it to suspend the gutted body of Lieutenant Boyle in mock crucifixion.

Quantico's sternly
modern space ...

It is not only gothic horror, but what has been termed the 'female gothic'[58] that is at work in *The Silence of the Lambs*. Like Starling, the heroine of the gothic romance finds herself within a strange landscape. For Tania Modleski,[59] the gothic novel is fundamentally contradictory, suggesting to women that they both should and should not be wary of male motivation. Perhaps more to the point, Mary Ann Doane cites Joanna Russ's description of the female gothic as 'adventure stories with passive protagonists'.[60] Of course Starling is by no means a passive figure; her status as an FBI agent (even if only temporary) defines her as an active, enquiring heroine. Where marriage, family or some other private

... and the Gothic space of the Baltimore asylum

'What did you see Clarice?': Lecter seems to mesmerise Starling in their final meeting

circumstance may take the heroine of the gothic romance, Starling is taken by her professional quest. Nonetheless Starling's investigation leads her through a series of iconographically distinct and threatening worlds: the asylum itself; the Baltimore storage facility where she uncovers Raspeil's head; the site of Lecter's improvised Memphis cell; and, finally, Buffalo Bill's basement itself. As in the gothic then, horror and danger for the female protagonist is associated as much with place as with individuals or institutions. Any such distinction is difficult to draw with certainty, however, since the spaces that Starling travels through so clearly function as externalised representations of the killer's world: place is peculiarly invested with meaning and value.

There is a more particular version of the woman's film that we can consider here, however: the 1940s' cycle inflected by horror and film noir that Doane refers to as the 'paranoid woman's film', part of a larger group of narratives which make up the female gothic. (Among the Hollywood titles that Doane discusses in this context are Hitchcock's *Rebecca* [1940] and *Suspicion* [1941], *The Spiral Staircase* [Robert Siodmak, 1946], *Secret Beyond the Door* [Fritz Lang, 1948] and *Caught* [Max Ophuls, 1949]). The paranoia that Doane refers to relates to a 'scenario in which the wife invariably fears that her husband is planning to kill her'. She is often correct, so that these are films in which 'the institution of marriage is haunted by murder'.[61] Although she is a rather passive player in the mystery that is played out around her, the heroine must learn to question appearances and to look for hidden secrets. Just so, Starling makes her way through threatening spaces, grappling with the puzzles that Lecter sets for her.

The deployment of space is crucial to the paranoid woman's film. Doane identifies three key recurrent figures here – stairs, doors and windows. Like hallways and corridors, all three are also threshold spaces. Transitional in some way, they are spaces that link to other spaces but which hold their own threats and possibilities. Both horror and the thriller exploit our capacity to imagine such possibilities to the full, emphasising our awareness of off-screen space, of what might emerge at any moment. Threshold spaces are points of departure as well as arrival. Think of how

Starling is repeatedly framed in doorways …

… and glimpsed in transitional spaces

often we see Starling in such spaces: the asylum corridor where she sits to speak with Lecter; the car park; the airport; the funeral home anteroom where she is left standing by Crawford; the storage facility where she must crawl under the door (that she cuts herself in the process reinforces, albeit in a small way, the danger of such adventures). Starling's response to being left out of things in the funeral home is to approach yet another set of doors, ones which lead in this instance to her past.

The parallel editing of Starling's arrival at Buffalo Bill's home against Crawford's assault on an empty house intensifies the charge involved in the film's imagery of doors as thresholds. Within the improbable geography of Gumb's home with its many basement rooms, Starling's challenge is both to unlock the secret behind the door and to shed light on Bill's crimes. She has already uncovered motive – something that Crawford and his team seem to care relatively little about at this stage. It is the crossing of this last threshold that instigates the film's most explicitly gothic scene in which Starling explores the secrets of this old, dark house. This sequence takes us fairly explicitly into a different kind of movie, with Starling now a composite of the victim-investigator of the woman's film and the victim-heroine of horror. Such a shift did not go unnoticed by critics. After Lecter's escape, says one, the film becomes 'very ordinary melodrama' with Starling 'just one more lady-in-jeopardy'.[62] While the confrontation may be melodramatic, it is hardly ordinary.

Hitchcock looms large over *The Silence of the Lambs*. Several years earlier Demme had aimed to make a Hitchcockian thriller in *Last Embrace* (US, 1979). While this endeavour was generally considered a failure, critics felt that with *Silence* Demme had succeeded in striking a balance between identification and suspense in the manner of Hitchcock's best thrillers. Demme distances himself from the emptiness of homage: 'I've embraced it [the Hitchcock style] more and more in my own quiet way, not necessarily in terms of visual flamboyance but more in the use of subjective camera and how to photograph actors to communicate story and character points.'[63] The most obvious reference point in Hitchcock's repertoire is of course the horror classic *Psycho* (US, 1960). The combination of modern and gothic settings in *Psycho*'s old, dark house on the hill and the more contemporary Bates Motel, the killer's transitional sexual identity (like Buffalo Bill, Norman Bates was based in part on Ed Gein) and the psychological explanations that don't really convince – all can be seen as informing *The Silence of the Lambs*. *Psycho* even features women with aspirations: doomed Marion and plucky Lila, a prototype amateur investigator and woman in peril. Yet just as pertinent for a discussion of Demme's *Silence* is Hitchcock's 1940 adaptation of Daphne Du Maurier's *Rebecca*, the film which Doane cites as launching the paranoid woman's film cycle.

   Rebecca delivers mystery and gothic romance, an old, dark house and a mysterious male romantic lead. The film centres on Joan Fontaine's character, who is never named. An orphan, she is working in Monte Carlo as the paid companion of an ungrateful and rather stupid older woman, when she meets and marries the mysterious Maxim de Winter (Laurence Olivier), returning with him to his vast family estate. The house, Manderley, is seemingly haunted by the ghost of Rebecca, the first Mrs de Winter. Fearful and timid, Fontaine can't seem to assert herself as mistress of the house. The resentful, deranged house-keeper Mrs Danvers plays mind games with her, attacking Fontaine's vulnerabilities about whether or not she really belongs. The story of a woman's struggle to assert her identity in an unfriendly context of male-dominated institutions, *The Silence of the Lambs* functions at times like a transplantation of the paranoid woman's film – with its threatening version of the domestic – to the very different, and very public context of the workplace. Pam Cook[64] views *Blue Steel* as a woman's film in precisely this context, although both romance and sexual threat are ironically much more central to Bigelow's film (Curtis's rookie cop Megan is first seduced and later raped by the killer she pursues). Both *Blue Steel*'s Megan and *Silence*'s Clarice are outsiders, framed by a generic uncertainty around the extent to which they belong.

   Starling's confident and purposeful manner cannot easily be equated with Joan Fontaine's girlish investigations of Manderley in *Rebecca*. Her anxieties and inexperience are a different matter. And, like

Rebecca: Joan Fontaine is overwhelmed by the Gothic space of Manderley

the implicitly lesbian Mrs Danvers, mind games are Lecter's chief weapons. The quickness with which he observes that Clarice is 'not real FBI' points up the extent to which both legitimacy and belonging are at issue in the film (not least of course its own legitimacy as upmarket horror). Lecter's goal might not be to drive Clarice Starling mad, as does the demonic husband in *Gaslight* (US, George Cukor, 1944) but he is set on playing with her mind – right down to his final phone call.

Modleski writes that 'Gothics are never about women who experience delusions of grandeur and omnipotence'. Instead, 'the Gothic heroine always feels helpless, confused, frightened and despised'.[65] The Clarice Starling we encounter in *The Silence of the Lambs* is perhaps a persecuted heroine, but she is not a paranoid one in this sense. Ironic perhaps, since the trajectory of both Harris's novel and Ridley Scott's film *Hannibal* is that 'they' really are out to get her. Starling's success, lovingly mapped by Demme in *The Silence of the Lambs*, triggers resentment and jealousy in the follow-up. The edgy malice of Harris's writing shows through as FBI Director, Tunberry, tells Starling's former mentor Jack Crawford, now on the brink of mandatory retirement, that 'a meat sacrifice' is called for. 'Fresh bleating meat' is required, but that 'they just might be satisfied with poultry … we can give them Clarice Starling and they'll leave us alone'.[66]

'Starling', Harris tells us in *Hannibal*, 'survived most of her life in institutions, by respecting them and playing hard and well by the rules. She had always advanced, won the scholarship, made the team. Her failure to advance in the FBI after a brilliant start was a new and awful experience for her. She batted against the glass ceiling like a bee in a bottle.'[67] No surprise perhaps that Scott pictures Starling in a dingy basement replaying past conversations with Lecter. An analogous pattern can be found in Cornwell's

Starling waits in Chilton's office; West Virginia law enforcement as seen from Starling's point of view

fiction, despite Scarpetta's glittering career. Almost all the Scarpetta novels feature the heroine coming up against obstructive individuals who resent her position of power. In one she is even threatened with indictment. In many she is threatened by the system within which she works as well as by the killer, whether personally or by proxy – she is then both victim(ised) and investigator. There is perhaps a sort of narcissism at work here since, as Modleski notes of the gothic novel, being 'persecuted ... is better than being ignored'.[68] Viewers of contemporary cinema are certainly familiar enough with stories of persecuted and ultimately triumphant males. And Scarpetta is both a powerful and a persecuted figure; both putative victim and investigator, she is always at the centre of the fiction, even when she is institutionally marginalised.

Starling's struggles with incompetent or indifferent authority figures in *The Silence of the Lambs* – Dr Chilton at the asylum, local law enforcement in West Virginia, even Crawford at times – are also staples of crime fiction. She is forced to operate as an independent, slipping through security for one last meeting with Lecter. Excluded from the big-guns FBI raid on Gumb's empty house in Chicago, Starling ends up tackling the villain/monster alone in a heroic confrontation that returns us once more to the iconography of the horror film.

If *The Silence of the Lambs* functions as a gothic woman's picture as much as gothic horror, Lecter occupies the place of the charming but mysterious and potentially violent gothic male ('People will say we're in love'). There is certainly a charge between the two, evident in the one brief moment of physical contact when Lecter's finger caresses Starling's as she clutches the case-file he passes to her. For one reviewer, Lecter is to Starling 'both perverse father-substitute and the demon-lover who submits her to psychological rape as the price of his assistance'.[69] Lecter does twice quiz Starling on the character of her relationships with older men – speculating whether Crawford fantasises about her sexually, and later asking if the rancher with whom she had stayed for such a short time had sexually abused her. Yet their relationship is of a different sort, defined by a mutual fascination as much as by power games: as Starling tells Lecter in response to his sexual innuendo, 'That doesn't interest me.'

Public and private worlds are very much interdependent in *The Silence of the Lambs*: the film's complexity lies in the intricate folding together of the two. Starling's pursuit of Buffalo Bill is linked to her desire for public success (Lecter tells her that it is 'advancement' which she loves most) but also to her quest for peace from her memories of the screaming lambs. *The Silence of the Lambs* is also in this way a rites of passage narrative with the inexperienced but knowledgeable and intuitive Starling in an eroticised student/teacher relationship with Lecter. Pursuit is a doubly charged love affair, since catching Gumb will bring Starling professional success. She has, we might note, no interest in 'understanding' Lecter, being more interested in picking his brains.

5 Under the Skin

Despite the fact that the film's psychiatrist is an anti-hero at best (and insane to boot), like Hitchcock's *Psycho*, *The Silence of the Lambs* shows itself to be keenly aware of both popular psychology and psychoanalysis (in Harris's novel, Lecter refers to the latter as a 'dead religion').[70] The work of investigation and of (psycho)analysis fold into each other as the film's narrative develops. This is most obviously the case in Lecter's trading of clues in return for an invasive look at Starling's buried memories of childhood trauma. Self-knowledge and knowledge of the case are intimately linked for Starling as Lecter's first pun/clue – 'Look deep within *your*self' – suggests.

The critical response to *The Silence of the Lambs* was also heavily informed by psychoanalysis (popular and otherwise). And if there is one figure that recurs again and again in discussions of the film, it is the father. Clarice's relationship with Lecter and Crawford has been widely read as paternalistic – they are seen as representing bad and good fathers respectively. For Martha Gever, Starling's 'heroic trajectory is plotted by a pantheon of fathers'.[71] It is true that Hollywood, when it has time for adventurous young women at all, tends to emphasise their relationship to their fathers: think of Jodie Foster as Ellie in *Contact* (US, Robert Zemeckis, 1997), whose encounter with an alien takes the form of a conversation with her father, or Helen Hunt as Jo in *Twister* (US, Jan de Bont, 1996), a scientist whose pursuit of tornados is framed by the loss of her father during a storm. Yet, although Lecter and Crawford are both figures of authority, there is no reason to assume that they are father figures. Taken to extremes, almost any male figure can be read as paternal. David Sundelson finds failing, dangerous or would-be fathers everywhere in the film from Dr Chilton to Mr Bimmel: for him the scene in which Starling asserts herself over the various police officers gathered around the body in the funeral home functions as if she were 'banishing a roomful of fathers so that she can do their work by herself'.[72]

At two key moments of emotional intensity there *are* flashbacks to the young Clarice and her town marshal father. The first follows Starling's initial

Lecter caresses
Starling's finger in their
one moment of physical
contact

'Your father would have
been proud today':
Crawford congratulates
Special Agent Starling

meeting with Lecter. Emerging from the horror of the asylum into the
brightness of daylight, Starling walks towards her rather battered car. The
familiar point-of-view shot transports us to the perspective of the young
Clarice, attempting to surprise her father as he arrives home. He spots her,
greets her and the two delightedly embrace. Her question, 'Did you get any
bad guys today, Daddy?' and his response – 'No angel, they all got away' –
sets up a failing that the adult Starling will aim to remedy. Accents, costume
and *mise en scène* all confirm with quiet economy the accuracy of Lecter's
comments on Starling's poor West Virginian origins (just as her car tells us
that she is still on a budget). Indeed we can speculate that these very
comments have in some way been responsible for summoning up this
memory of her father. Equally, the second flashback, which takes place at the
funeral home in West Virginia, emphasises Starling's origins – her career in
law enforcement has taken her back to her home state. Left in the anteroom
by Crawford, Starling seems drawn towards the simple funeral service taking

Starling recalls her father

Crawford shields Starling from the press

place in the room beyond. Mesmerised, Starling seems to walk towards the casket, the shaky camera indicating her emotion. A cut takes us back once more to the young Clarice, here silently contemplating her father's body. The sounds of the moment intrude on Starling's memory, pulling her and us back to the present and the body of Buffalo Bill's victim.

The father/daughter relationship is certainly important to *Silence*'s elaboration of Clarice Starling's character. Her college success and career in the FBI have taken her away from her past and into a very different professional world. Yet at the same time she is a sort of cop and this simultaneously binds her to her past through her father. It is not, then, that the father is an insignificant figure in the film. But it would be a mistake to read Clarice Starling's development as all about this one relationship. Lecter diagnoses Starling early on as ambitious; her cure is not to run back to Daddy, but to take his place. Solving the case – and saving Catherine Martin – offers a fantasy of completion and resolution that both lays childhood memories to rest and allows her to take her place of responsibility and authority in the world.

Interestingly, Harris's novel has Starling summon the memory of her mother to bring her strength as she asks the deputies to leave the room: 'Clarice Starling, standing at the sink, needed now a prototype of courage more apt and powerful than any Marine parachute jump. The image came to her, and helped her, but it pierced her too: *Her mother, standing at the sink, washing blood out of her father's hat, running cold water over the hat, saying, "We'll be all right, Clarice. Tell your brothers and sister to wash up and come to the table. We need to talk and then we'll fix our supper."*'[73]

Harris seems determined to sabotage the very idea of the father, refusing the obviousness of the father/daughter relationship as an 'explanation' for his protagonist's actions. Instead Harris constructs alternative sets of relationships between characters, from the cop/killer double (of which more in a moment) to other couples that displace the father/daughter relationship – mother and daughter, brother and sister, even husband and wife. In *Hannibal* too, Starling is at times construed as Lecter's bride and at times as a surrogate sister, replacement for the lost Mischa.

When it comes to powerful women, popular literature seems happy enough to buy into a circuit of symbolic fathers, at least superficially. Cornwell's Scarpetta tells us in *Cruel and Unusual*: 'In a sense, I had become my father after he died. I was the rational one who made A's and knew how to cook and handle money. I was the one who rarely cried and whose reaction to the volatility in my disintegrating home was to cool down and disperse like a vapour.'[74] In the earlier *Body of Evidence* Scarpetta confesses that: 'The career I had embarked on would forever return me to the scene of the terrible crime of my father's death.'[75] In her first novel featuring forensic anthropologist Dr Temperance Brennan, Kathy Reichs has her heroine recall her therapist's cautionary words: 'you are the child of an alcoholic father. You are searching for the attention he denied you. You want Daddy's approval, so you try to please everybody.'[76] Daddy is certainly a presence in the back-story of both characters. Yet the most significant relationships are not with these remembered fathers but with daughters, nieces and female friends. Indeed over the course of the Scarpetta novels, it is the protagonist's brilliant and beautiful lesbian niece Lucy who becomes the most developed figure of fantasised achievement.

Alluring though its answers might be, the trouble with psychoanalysis, it seems, is its insistence on the power of the paternal figure (an insistence that works to obscure other elements which might be just as central). Other popular discourses of gender and sexual identity also make their mark in fiction and film. In *The Body Farm*, Scarpetta expresses her nature in crudely gendered terms: 'I was the body and sensibilities of a woman with the power and drive of a man.'[77] As Janet Staiger writes in relation to the reception of *Silence*, the common sense of stereotypes in US cinema (and indeed, common-sense versions of psychoanalysis) tell us that 'a strong woman must be a lesbian'.[78] For Staiger this conflation fed into and subtly supported the outing campaign against Foster. Equally, of course, the common sense of stereotypes suggests that a man with any kind of investment in femininity must be gay – an interpretation that certainly fed into the debates around the characterisation of Buffalo Bill.

It is in the charismatic figure of the insane psychiatrist Hannibal Lecter that *The Silence of the Lambs* most obviously expresses an ambivalence about those who study or work with the mind. Both physically repellent and emotionally threatening, capable of careful, even elegant reasoning while evidently insane, Lecter embodies a contemporary twist on the mad scientist of horror and science-fiction. As an unscrupulous but gifted psychiatrist he invades the most private dreams and fantasies. It is a convention – even a cliché – of crime fiction and crime cinema that the cop and his suspect are similar creatures, perhaps even doubles. They understand each other in an intense, special way, and this understanding allows the investigator to catch his or her opponent. Yet it also sets the investigator apart; it could even drive him or her temporarily insane, as with Will Graham in Harris's *Red Dragon*. Jack Crawford warns Starling about the perils of involvement before her very first meeting with Lecter ('You're to tell him nothing personal'). As reason slips into unreason, analysis into magic, the profiler and his subject meet, calling into question the boundary between them while emphasising the superior sensitivity of both.

The twist in *The Silence of the Lambs* is to conflate the twin figures of reason and of unreason more completely, so that Lecter is both perverse profiler and psychopath. While in *Manhunter* Will Graham conducts a battle of wills with Lecter, in *The Silence of the Lambs* Lecter is both killer and investigator. Lecter's gift is to see clearly what others miss, to notice the ways in which day-to-day behaviour involves a staging of human desires. If anything, his insight is heightened by his physical confinement. Indeed, the one occasion on which he fails to see, when his judgment is clouded, is associated with the false offer made by Starling of a temporary escape.

As much as *The Silence of the Lambs* appeals to reason, to psychology, deductive logic and physical evidence, insanity and the figure of the psychopath underpin the narrative, embodied in the idea of the serial killer. Perpetrator of horrific crimes, largely committed against strangers, the psychopath seems to exceed explanation. 'Psychologists call him a psychopath – they don't know what else to call him,' says Will Graham of Lecter in *Manhunter*. Yet – in the form of Lecter – the psychopath can offer explanation for others. A monstrous and fascinating

Lecter as erudite profiler ...

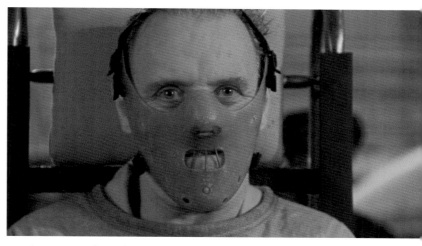

… and as monstrous figure of malice

threat, the serial killer is now as familiar a type as his cinematic counterpart, the wise, intuitive profiler. Both the threat and the promise are implicit in the very introduction of Lecter which neatly segues from Crawford's windowless Quantico office to that of Dr Chilton (more opulent, with its wood panelling) at the asylum. 'Just do your job but never forget what he is,' deadpans Crawford in extreme close-up. 'And what is that?' asks the inquisitive Starling. The response – 'Oh, he's a monster, pure psychopath' – comes from Chilton. Starling stands uncomfortably in front of him – perhaps the twittering of birds that underlies his first words is a sign of her trepidation? To Chilton, Lecter is a specimen: 'I keep him in here,' he tells Starling with a flourish. Yet the smarmy Chilton is clearly something of a fool – a self-interested showman rather than the voice of authority that his title or his position might suggest: labels, we may feel, fail to tell us a great deal.

Both the police procedural and the psychological thriller offer the spectacle of reason in pursuit of madness, yet no insight is ever offered into Lecter's pathology (there is, not entirely successfully, an attempt to provide this in Harris's *Hannibal*). The quest to gain such an insight is the ostensible reason for Starling's very first encounter with Lecter, although the subject quickly turns the tables, sneering at the crudities of the FBI's tools for classifying criminal behaviours. In the face of insanity, *The Silence of the Lambs* offers the idea of the serial killer as a sort of talisman. The serial killer may be insane but he is methodical; he has a ritual and his crimes involve a signature.

Though Lecter is scathing about labels – hence the famous line about eating a census taker's liver – he tacitly accepts that of 'serial killer' in the following exchange. 'Why do you think he [Buffalo Bill] removes their skins, Agent Starling? Thrall me with your acumen.' 'It excites him. Most serial killers keep some sort of trophies from their victims.' 'I didn't.' 'No. No, you ate yours.' Though accepting that he can be defined as a serial killer, Lecter also subtly emphasises his unique qualities here, the extent to which he does *not* fit the pattern. When Starling challenges Lecter to see himself with the kind of precise (indeed cruel) insight he has shown in relation to her, he responds first by rejecting her ('You fly back to school now, little Starling') and then, in subsequent meetings, by turning the spotlight on to her desires and memories rather than his motives.

The popular image of the serial killer is that of a compulsive individual who acts out a secret fantasy, a violent man nonetheless capable of intricate planning or perhaps simply animal cunning. Serial killers have become figures of fascination within popular cinema, partly in service of a gruesome voyeurism, but also because they foreground questions of motive in relation to seemingly random acts of violence – why these particular victims and not others, for instance. The fascination of the serial killer is not just to do with random killing, though the cruelty of the luckless victims' fates plays a part. The serial killer dehumanises the individual – his victims are simply lesser animals within a hierarchy of which he is the pinnacle. In this the serial killer has been seen as a figure of modernity: anonymous behind a mask of impassivity, he is geographically mobile, protected by the 'invisibility' of white masculinity. By contrast, as we've seen, Starling sees the victims as individuals, rehumanising them as it were.

We've seen that the detective narrative emphasises explanation, while horror mobilises evil or the supernatural. As a hybrid of these two

Lecter's sudden
violence …

… is followed by a
return to calm

genres, *The Silence of the Lambs* offers us two distinct versions of the serial killer. On the one hand he is a madman, inhabiting his own peculiar world with its rituals, symbols and value systems. On the other hand, he is a monster – a figure of evil. Both are outcasts, figures of otherness whose function is to reassure us about our own sanity and goodness. The construction of the serial killer as monstrous in *The Silence of the Lambs*, or in films such as *The Bone Collector* or *The Cell*, is not completely at odds with an explanatory narrative (whether psychological or otherwise). In horror, a genre of sequels, the monster has its own mythology, and plays (after a fashion) by agreed rules. Crucifix, silver bullet, stake through the heart: myth may provide the monsters, but it may equally suggest strategies – or perhaps heroic individuals – to ensure their demise. In serial killer mythology, as we've seen, an abused childhood often provides an explanation for the killer's origins. The key to finding him is to understand his ritual, to locate the signature that will reveal all. Violence is methodical

The serial killer as animalistic: Eugene (Ron Silver) in *Blue Steel*

not mindless in *The Silence of the Lambs*. Gumb wants to become other than he is, a transformation he pursues literally and doggedly; Lecter wants a view, his escape is thus a means to an end, while the suggestion that he will kill Chilton is clearly motivated by his treatment in the asylum. Nonetheless, the violence exceeds what is strictly 'necessary' – society suggests that we seek contentment or physical transformation in other ways (although we are informed that Bill has applied for society's version of gender reassignment and been rejected).

Like Lecter's elegant but deranged scientist, a characterisation that alludes to figures of nineteenth-century horror including Frankenstein, Jekyll and Hyde, and even Dracula, Buffalo Bill is also a hybrid figure. Based on elements from three killers, Ed Gein, Ted Bundy and Gary Heidnik, Bill is also a composite of previous movie serial killers – *Psycho*'s Norman Bates, most obviously – and of stereotypes found in popular

The serial killer's identity is a shifting, transitional one: *Psycho*'s voyeuristic, mother-fixated Norman Bates (Anthony Perkins) provides a prototype for Buffalo Bill

media coverage of the true crime variety. While we can usefully understand the serial killer as a 'phenomenon of modern ... and advanced societies',[79] he is also a mythical figure. Indeed, both Thomas Harris and Ted Tally seem to have drawn as freely on myth and on fairy tales as on behavioural psychology, forensic medicine and contemporary cases.

With Buffalo Bill, *Silence* emphasises deviance rather than the calculating madness that characterises Lecter. Buffalo Bill's victims are all big; they fail to meet the physical ideals of white womanhood (despite attempts: we see a diet book among other personal possessions in Fredericka's bedroom). Rather distasteful then that Orion's press release for *The Silence of the Lambs* tells us that Catherine 'is held captive in Buffalo Bill's basement while he waits for her to *lose weight*'. Bill's starvation of his victims perhaps represents an attempt to shape them into his preferred version of femininity – literally, it may function to aid the process of flaying, but it is also bound up with the exercise of his power to give and withhold life. With the sole exception of the affluent Catherine Martin, the one who gets away (and who shows evident ingenuity), Bill preys on working-class women – women defined by their relative lack of economic power. Only Catherine with her powerful mother is, it seems, significant enough to mobilise the FBI into action.

Hannibal Lecter, while by agreement a monster, is defiantly high-culture: confined to his cell he sketches Florence from memory and maintains his manners, with Starling at least (there are evidently limits to his self-conscious courtesy however). His cannibalism makes him a dangerous predator, but he is explicitly presented as savage in only one sequence – the bloody escape from his Memphis cell. Even here, the Bach underlines the Doctor's class, or at least his taste. Perversely, even Lecter's cannibalism seems almost refined when set against Buffalo Bill's skinning of women – a gourmet seeking out the culinary exotic, he incorporates others rather than attempting to get inside them.

Just as Lecter's command of culture sets off Gumb's more lumpen characterisation, his intelligence and vision serve to underscore Chilton's fatally limited insight. Moreover Lecter's insistence on courtesy – appealing at a distance, whatever his proclivities – contrasts with Chilton's

Miggs embodies madness as sexual aggression and lack of control

clumsy attempts to hit on Starling at their first meeting. In Lecter's cultured bogeyman, *Silence* provides a seemingly rational figure whom we nonetheless know to be insane. Of course Lecter is not insane after the usual movie fashion. Witness the other inmates in the Baltimore asylum: Multiple Miggs (as Lecter dismissively terms him), animalistic in his sexual aggression, or those listed in the credits simply as 'friendly psychopath' and 'brooding psychopath'. Each is defined by traits of a basic kind – their madness is apparent in their simplicity as much as anything else. Lecter, by contrast, is defined by complexity, by restraint and self-control – he withholds information (where Bill withholds food) and controls language. The people he meets cannot, it seems, help giving themselves away in the small details of their dress and mannerisms. Starling, with her good bag and cheap shoes, aspires to taste and believes that hard work will be rewarded. Lecter discerns both her achievements and her self-doubt, playing on both to his own ends.

The contradictions of Lecter's persona – 'charming psychopath' we might dub him – helped make him a cause célèbre on the film's initial release. For some reviewers, Lecter's cultured tastes suggested an endorsement of his violence. He is just *too* charming. Peculiar that we do not seem to think that the reverse might equally apply – that Lecter's savagery might question the culture to which he lays claim (and which Starling desires so badly). Yet critics heaped praise on Hopkins for his performance, emphasising the role it played in giving the film a distinction not usually found in horror: 'he does it all without weapons of destruction or any of the rest of the horror movie accoutrements. Nevertheless, he has extraordinary tools – his face and his voice.'[80]

Lecter's appeal lies in his elaborate courtesy towards Starling and his contemptuous rejection of the very authority that, as a supposedly learned man, he represents. Ultimately audiences can enthusiastically endorse Lecter's contempt for Chilton, enjoying the joke of the film's closing moments. To Anthony Lane, Lecter is 'Holmes and Moriarty in one, scornful of all the Watsons in the world'.[81] Lecter has both the brilliance and the coldness of Holmes, who once confided to Watson that he would have made an excellent criminal should he have chosen to pursue that route. Lecter's uncanny ability to deduce events and emotions from scents and other slight clues ('Your bleeding has stopped,' he observes to Starling, unprompted) certainly recalls Holmes's pleasure in bewildering visitors with his knowledge of their position in life or their recent activities ('I have found it wise to impress clients with a sense of power,'[82] muses Holmes). Knowledge is power in this context – something that Starling realises when she attempts to turn Lecter's own weapons against him.

Popular narratives typically operate through a series of thematic oppositions – in *Silence* these include reason and madness, above and below ground, night and day, masculine and feminine. Yet these are rarely preserved for the duration of the telling of any tale – it is, after all, in the transgression of such oppositions that the interest of story-telling lies. Horror and fantasy offer a plethora of figures that transgress oppositions: border-crossing creatures of one kind or another. Vampires are both living

Lecter as charming psychopath

and dead, werewolves both human and animal. Moreover, the werewolf repeatedly enacts its transition from human to animal (as do variants of the Jekyll and Hyde narrative – with its proto-Ripper formula – from socially correct to animalistic humanity). Conversely, on her death the female vampire is typically transformed from sexual undead to virginal corpse, thus becoming human (or at least woman) once more. Lecter is compared to a vampire at one point, an appropriately aristocratic monster (in Harris's novel, Starling feels 'suddenly empty, as though she had given blood'[83] during her first meeting with Lecter).

In terms of horror archetypes, Buffalo Bill is something of a perverse composite of Frankenstein and his monstrous creation, stitching together a new skin that will no more serve to provide an integrated social identity than the bride whom Frankenstein constructs (and then destroys) for his monster. Elsewhere, Bill is animalistic – he stalks and sets traps for his prey. Bill is most explicitly human and animal simultaneously when he impersonates Catherine Martin's screams, pulling his vest out in front of him as if he had a woman's breasts. We've already seen that metaphors of transformation play a central part in *The Silence of the Lambs*, expressed in a rich imagery of winged creatures. Elsewhere I have characterised both Starling and Gumb as cross-dressers;[84] Gumb's perverse attempt to construct a female body can be compared with Starling's cross-class aspirations and the investment that she makes in masculinity (to the extent that agency and authority are coded masculine). Thus the two are an apt pairing: Buffalo Bill is a man with an investment in femininity (something of

Buffalo Bill's mimicry of Catherine Martin's screams

a perverse ambition, the film seems to suggest), while Starling is a woman whose actions are framed by masculine terms. Yet Gumb's nickname emphasises a masculine heritage, while the characterisation of Starling is so powerful partly because she is a transitional rather than a one-dimensional figure: both heroic and vulnerable. Border-crossing is a characteristic of heroic as well as monstrous figures.

While Starling's aspirations are validated, heroic in the context of the film, Gumb's, and I would argue Lecter's, are monstrous, pathological and destructive. Even so, the monstrous may be appealing: Lecter is a compelling villain. We've already seen that he exceeds explanation ('he's a monster'). As a cannibal he literally ingests his victims, breaking a fundamental cultural taboo. Staiger draws our attention to the repeated puns that contemporary reviewers made on taste and on food when writing about the film,[85] almost as if Lecter's cannibalism is a source of pleasure, acting out a taboo fantasy that appeals – or certainly fascinates – as much as it repels.

In one sense, Lecter's insane self-possession operates as a perverse commentary on western culture's quest for self-knowledge. Therapies, fitness kicks and self-help regimes are so many avoidance strategies in the face of the slab: Starling's desire for advancement, Gumb's wish for transformation, Fredericka Bimmel's ambitions of a big city job. And overlaying it all is the abiding preoccupation of talk-shows and self-help manuals: gender and sexual identity. No surprise then that the film was simultaneously regarded as a feminist milestone and a worrying articulation of homophobic panic.

The Silence of the Lambs locates its narrative, even its terror, in the uncertainties produced by social change, as ideas about what men and women are, and what we should or could be, constantly shift and evolve. What does it mean to be a man, to be a woman, to follow one's desires? Lecter and Buffalo Bill both literalise their fantasies through their victims (Lecter's sense of superiority is evident in his consumption of human flesh; Bill's aspirations are directed to shaping and wearing the flesh of his victims). Starling's aspirations – indeed her development through the course of the film – are of a different sort. The story of Bluebeard, perhaps the most obvious fairy tale to which *The Silence of the Lambs* owes a debt, is a useful reference point in this context. Bluebeard tells his new wife that she may open any door in the castle but one. Unable to restrain her curiosity, she disobeys her husband, finding a bloody secret in the hidden chamber – the murdered wives who went before her, and who she must now join.[86] Through its questing female protagonist, *Silence* re-presents the imagery of Bluebeard as a parable of male violence rather than a cautionary tale about keeping to one's place, in the process investing the serial killer narrative with a distinctive contemporary resonance.

Drawing together psychology, profiling and forensic pathology, *The Silence of the Lambs* makes a bid to read off identity and motive from action, behaviour and from the body itself (whether living or dead). At the same time, the film offers up monsters, desires and actions that seem inexplicable. Yet horror and investigation are not in conflict here, mediated as they both are by the themes and narrative devices of the woman's picture. *The Silence of the Lambs* typifies a cinematic – indeed a cultural – preoccupation with getting under the skin, whether through the tools of science or brutal violence. Scientific disciplines and criminal violence each open the mind and body to expert scrutiny, whether malevolent or benign.

Jame Gumb at work

Notes

1 Thomas Harris, *The Silence of the Lambs* (1988; London: Mandarin, 1999), p. 196.
2 Ibid., p. 215.
3 Amy Taubin, 'Killing Men', *Sight and Sound* vol. 1 no. 1 (NS), May 1991, p. 18.
4 Though Harris has the pair living a fantastic existence in South America, the movie keeps Starling firmly in the FBI camp at its close.
5 Gavin Smith, 'Identity Check', interview with Jonathan Demme, *Film Comment* vol. 27 no. 1, January/February 1991, p. 29.
6 Harris, *Silence*, pp. 281–2.
7 Ibid., p. 302.
8 Ibid., p. 303.
9 Ibid., p. 204.
10 Ibid., p. 346.
11 Cited in Smith, 'Identity Check', pp. 29–30.
12 Mike Nichols's *Working Girl* (US, 1988) and Steven Soderbergh's *Erin Brockovich* (US, 2000) are two – very different – recent exceptions.
13 Jeanine Basinger, *A Woman's View: How Hollywood Spoke to Women 1930–1960* (Hanover, CT: Wesleyan University Press, 1993).
14 B. Ruby Rich, 'Nobody's Handmaid', *Sight and Sound* vol. 1 no. 8 (NS), December 1991, p. 8.
15 Cited in Smith, 'Identity Check', p. 30.
16 Although the rather disappointing *V. I. Warshawski*, starring Kathleen Turner as Paretsky's PI heroine, was released in July 1991, a few months after *The Silence of the Lambs*.
17 There are also of course comedies, from a minor movie like *Feds* (US, Dan Goldberg, 1989) to the box-office smash *Miss Congeniality* (US, Donald Petrie, 2000) in which Sandra Bullock's tomboy FBI agent goes undercover at a beauty pageant.
18 *The Silence of the Lambs*, *Copycat*, *Seven*, *Kiss the Girls*, *The Bone Collecter*: none had summer releases.
19 Carol J. Clover, *Men, Women and Chainsaws: Gender in the Modern Horror Film* (Princeton, NJ: Princeton University Press, 1992), p. 20.
20 Nancy Drew first appeared in 1930 in 'The Secret of the Old Clock'. She has since become something of a publishing industry. Warner Bros. made several short Nancy Drew films in the late 1930s.
21 Daniel O'Brien, *The Hannibal Files* (London: Reynolds & Hearn, 2001), p. 81.
22 Ibid., p. 77.
23 Michael Bliss and Christina Banks, *What Goes Around Comes Around: The Films of Jonathan Demme* (Carbondale: Southern Illinois University Press, 1996), p. 143.
24 *Empire*, February 2000, p.44.
25 Clover, *Men, Women and Chainsaws*, p. 232.
26 Ibid., p. 236.
27 Richard Dyer, *Seven* (London: BFI Modern Classics, 1999), p. 73.
28 Bliss and Banks, *What Goes Around*, p. 141.
29 Smith, 'Identity Check', p. 29.
30 Clover, *Men, Women and Chainsaws*, p. 233.
31 Zea is speaking in 'Inside the Labyrinth: The Making of *The Silence of the Lambs*', a documentary which appears on the Special Edition DVD of *The Silence of the Lambs* (2001).
32 Tino Balio, *Grand Design: Hollywood as a Modern Business Enterprise, 1930–1939* (Los Angeles: University of California Press, 1993), p. 179.

33 Mark Seltzer, *Serial Killers: Death and Life in America's Wound Culture* (London: Routledge, 1998), p. 39.
34 Diana Fuss, *Identification Papers* (London: Routledge, 1995), p. 95.
35 See Taubin, 'Killing Men'. Taubin also contributes to 'Inside the Labyrinth'.
36 Stephen Harvey in 'Writers on the Lamb', *Village Voice*, 5 March 1991, p. 56.
37 Alison Darren's *Lesbian Film Guide* (London: Cassell, 2000) dubs *Basic Instinct* 'pure flash trash', politically troubling perhaps, but offering the opportunity to simply 'lie back and enjoy it' (p. 19).
38 B. Ruby Rich, 'Nobody's Handmaid', p. 10.
39 Michael Mustu, *Village Voice*, 28 January 1992, p. 48.
40 Brian Jarvis, 'Watching the Detectives: Body Images, Sexual Politics and Ideology in Contemporary Crime Film', in Peter Messent (ed.), *Criminal Proceedings: The Contemporary American Crime Novel* (London: Pluto, 1997), p. 223.
41 Cited in Messent, *Criminal Proceedings*, pp. 12–13.
42 Bliss and Banks, *What Goes Around*, p. 141.
43 Barbara Creed, *The Monstrous-Feminine: Film, Feminism, Psychoanalysis* (London: Routledge, 1993), p. 9.
44 Patricia Cornwell, *Postmortem* (London: Warner Books, 1990), pp. 91–2.
45 Edgar Allan Poe, 'The Murders in the Rue Morgue' (1845), in *The Fall of the House of Usher and Other Writings* (Harmondsworth: Penguin, 1986), p. 206.
46 Harris, *Silence*, pp. 278–9.
47 Harvey Roy Greenberg, 'Psychotherapy at the Simplex', *Journal of Popular Film and Television* vol. 20 no. 2, Summer 1992, p. 13.
48 Seltzer, *Serial Killers*, p. 4.
49 Ibid., p. 16. Robert K. Ressler, with Tom Shachtman, *Whoever Fights Monsters: My Twenty Years Tracking Serial Killers for the FBI* (New York: St Martin's Press, 1993); John E. Douglas and Mark Olshaker, *Mindhunter: Inside the FBI's Elite Serial Crime Unit* (New York: Simon & Schuster, 1995).
50 Cornwell, *Postmortem*, pp. 91–2.
51 Dyer, *Seven*, p. 9.
52 Seltzer, *Serial Killers*, p. 131.
53 Harris, *Silence*, p. 183.
54 Karen Halttunen, *Murder Most Foul: The Killer and the American Gothic Imagination* (Cambridge, MA: Harvard University Press, 1998), p. 53.
55 Ibid., p. 49.
56 Jonathan Demme interviewed by Ana Maria Bahiana, *Cinema Papers* no. 83, May 1991, p. 15.
57 Sir Arthur Conan Doyle, 'The Mazarin Stone' (1927) in *The Case-Book of Sherlock Holmes* (Harmondsworth: Penguin, 1986), p. 63. It is interesting to note that Holmes's comment is made in relation to food – he refuses to eat, asserting that the effort of digestion deprives the brain of its blood supply.
58 Mary Ann Doane, *The Desire to Desire: The Woman's Film of the 1940s* (London: Macmillan, 1987), p. 124.
59 Tania Modleski, *Loving with a Vengeance: Mass-Produced Fantasies for Women* (New York: Routledge, 1982), p. 64.
60 Doane, *The Desire to Desire*, p. 135.
61 Ibid., p. 123.
62 Alexander Walker, 'Unhealthy Appetite', *Evening Standard*, 30 May 1991, p. 26.
63 In Bliss and Banks, *What Goes Around*, p. 142.

64 Pam Cook, 'No Fixed Address: The Woman's Picture from *Outrage* to *Blue Steel*', in Steve Neale and Murray Smith (eds), *Contemporary Hollywood Cinema* (London: Routledge, 1998).

65 Modleski, *Loving with a Vengeance*, p. 65.

66 Thomas Harris, *Hannibal* (London: Heinemann, 1999), p. 24.

67 Ibid., p. 27.

68 Modleski, *Loving with a Vengeance*, p. 65.

69 Hugo Davenport, 'The Mythic Power of Hopkins' Modern Bluebeard', *Daily Telegraph*, 30 May 1991, p. 15.

70 Harris, *Silence*, p. 157.

71 Martha Gever in 'Writers on the Lamb', p. 49.

72 David Sundelson, 'The Demon Therapist and Other Dangers: Jonathan Demme's *The Silence of the Lambs*', *Journal of Popular Film and Television* vol. 21 no. 1, Spring 1993, pp. 12–17.

73 Harris, *Silence*, p. 78.

74 Patricia Cornwell, *Cruel and Unusual* (London: Warner, 1993), p. 397.

75 Patricia Cornwell, *Body of Evidence* (London: Warner, 1991), p. 161.

76 Kathy Reichs, *Déjà Dead* (London: Arrow, 1998), p. 40.

77 Patricia Cornwell, *The Body Farm* (London: Warner, 1994), p. 341.

78 Janet Staiger, 'Taboos and Totems: Cultural Meanings of *The Silence of the Lambs*', in Jim Collins, Hilary Radner and Ava Preacher Collins (eds), *Film Theory Goes to the Movies* (London: Routledge/AFI, 1993), p. 144.

79 Dyer, *Seven*, p. 37.

80 Ivor Davis, *Daily Mail*, 1 February 1991, p. 28.

81 Anthony Lane, 'Doctor Death', *Independent on Sunday*, 3 March 1991, p. 13.

82 Conan Doyle, 'The Adventure of the Blanched Soldier' (1926), in *The Case-Book of Sherlock Holmes*, p. 39.

83 Harris, *Silence*, p. 23.

84 Yvonne Tasker, *Working Girls: Gender and Sexuality in Popular Cinema* (London: Routledge, 1998).

85 Staiger reviews the US press, but British newspapers employed a similar repertoire: for instance, 'Horrors Supp'd with Gentleman's Relish' (*Independent on Sunday*, 2 June 1991) or 'Nice to Eat You' (*Guardian*, 30 May 1991).

86 In some versions of the tale, she is rescued from her grisly fate.

Credits

THE SILENCE OF THE LAMBS

USA
1990

Director
Jonathan Demme
Producers
Edward Saxon, Kenneth Utt,
Ron Bozman
Screenplay
Ted Tally
Based on the novel by
Thomas Harris
Director of Photography
Tak Fujimoto
Editor
Craig McKay
Production Designer
Kristi Zea
Music
Howard Shore

© Orion Pictures
Corporation
Production Companies
A Strong Heart/Demme
production
A Jonathan Demme picture
An Orion Pictures release
Executive Producers
Gary Goetzman
Associate Producer
Grace Blake
Financial Representative
Thomas A. Imperato
Production Auditor
Vicki Dee Rock

**Assistant Production
Auditor**
Steven Shareshian
Accounting Assistants
Katie Clarke, Ann Markel
**Assistant Production
Co-ordinators**
Lisa Bradley, Andrew
Sands, Alison Sherman
Unit Production Manager
Kenneth Utt
Location Co-ordinators
Washington DC:
John Crowder
Bimini, Bahamas:
Gus Holzer
Location Manager
Neri Kyle Tannenbaum
Locations
Annie Loeffler, Mike McCue
**Post-Production
Supervisor**
Marshall Persinger
**Post-Production
Assistants**
Sam Bruskin, Priscilla
Fleischman, Trish Breganti
Stage Manager
Paul Giorgi
Assistant to Mr Demme
Lucas Platt
Assistant to Mr Saxon
Valerie Thomas
Assistant to Mr Utt
Robin Fajardo
Assistant to Ms Foster
Pat LaMagna
**Special Production
Assistant**
Kevin McLeod

Production Assistants
Maria Mason, Gina White,
Becky Gibbs, Iane Ulan,
Monica Bielawski, Andre
Blake, Ben Ramsey, 'Buz'
Wasler, Hyle White, Paula
Oliver, Teri Hanson, Jeffrey
Barabe
1st Assistant Director
Ron Bozman
2nd Assistant Director
Kyle McCarthy
**2nd 2nd Assistant
Director**
Gina Leonetti
**Additional 1st Assistant
Director**
Steve Rose
Continuity
Mary A. Kelly
Casting
Howard Feuer
Pittsburgh Additional:
Donna Belajac
Pittsburgh Extras:
Staci Blagovich
Virginia Extras:
The Erickson Agency
Camera Operator
Tony Jannelli
1st Assistant Camera
Bruce MacCallum
2nd Assistant Camera
Tom O'Halloran
**Additional Camera
Assistants**
Larry Huston, Jay Levy
Camera Trainee
Brian Osmond

Steadicam Operator
Larry McConkey
Video Engineer
Howard Weiner
C-130 Aerial Sequences Filmed by
Cine/Exec Aviation Inc
Vectorvision by:
Nettmann
Pilots:
Jeff Senour, Jim Deeth
Camera Operator:
Mark Streapy
Technician:
Robert Vogt
Key Grip
Bill Miller
Dolly Grip
John Donohue
Grips
Matt Miller, Mick Lohrer,
Richard Aversa, Calvin Price
Gaffer
Rusty Engels
Best Boy Electric
Kenny Conners
Electricians
Mike Burke, Ed DeCort,
James Petri, Peter Demme,
Roswell Jones
Still Photographs by
Ken Regan
Special Effects
Dwight Benjamin-Creel
Associate Editor
Lisa Bromwell
1st Assistant Editor
Colleen Sharp

2nd Assistant Editor
Alice Stone
Apprentice Film Editors
David Kirkman, Lynn
Cassanti, Nzingha Clarke
Art Director
Tim Galvin
Art Department Co-ordinator
Francine Byrne
Assistant Art Directors
Natalie Wilson, Gary Kosko
Set Decorator
Karen O'Hara
Assistant Set Decorator
Diana L. Stoughton
Stand-by Dresser
C. A. Kelly
Set Dressers
Ken Turek, Ed Lohrer III,
Edward West
Storyboard Artists
Kalina Ivanov,
Karl Shefelman
Master Scenic Artist
Eileen Garrigan
Key Scenic Artist
Frederika Gray
Stand-by Scenic Artist/Special Drawings
Paula Payne
Property Master
Ann Miller
Assistant Props
Loren Levy, Sean Foyle
Construction Co-ordinator
S. Bruce Wineinger
Costume Designer
Colleen Atwood

Assistant Costume Designer
Kathleen Gerlach
Wardrobe Supervisors
Mark Burchard,
Hartsell Taylor
Wardrobe Assistant
Benjamin Wilson
Make-up Created by
Allen Weisinger
Special Make-up Effects Created by
Carl Fullerton, Neal Martz
Hair Styles Designed by
Alan D'Angerio
Main Titles Designed by
M&Co, NY
Titles/Optical Effects
R/Greenberg Associates,
Inc/NY
Colour Timing by
David Orr
Orchestrations by
Homer Denison
Music Supervision
Sharon Boyle
Music Editor
Suzana Periç
Assistant Music Editors
Nic Ratner, Sue Demskey
Recording Engineer
Alan Snelling
Soundtrack
'American Girl' by Tom Petty,
performed by Tom Petty and
the Heartbreakers; 'Sunny
Day' by T. Ottaviano,
performed by Book of Love;

'Goldberg Variations' by
J. S. Bach, performed by
Jerry Zimmerman; 'Hip
Priest' by M. E. Smith, M.
Riley, S. Hanley, C. Scanlon,
P. Hanley, performed by
The Fall; 'Alone' by Colin
Newman, G. Lewis,
performed by Colin
Newman; 'Real Men' by B.
Licher, M. Erskine, J. Long,
performed by Savage
Republic; 'Goodbye
Horses' by W. Garvey,
performed by Q. Lazzarus;
'Lanmo nan zile a'
by/performed by Les Frères
Parent
Sound Designer
Skip Lievsay
Production Sound Mixer
Christopher Newman
Sound Recordists
John Fundus
Boom Operator
Dennis Maitland II
Re-Recording Mixer
Tom Fleischman
Re-Recordists
Douglas L. Murray,
Sean Squires
Sound Mixed at
Sound One Corp/NY
Assistant Sound Editors
Anne Sawyer, Brian
Johnson
**Apprentice Sound
Editors**
Bill Docker, Stuart Levy,
Missy Cohen

Negative Matching by
J. G. Films, Inc
Dialogue Editors
Fred Rosenberg,
Jeffrey Stern,
Marissa Littlefield,
Phil Stockton
Effects Editors
Ron Bochar
ADR
Recordist:
David Boulton
Boom Operator:
Kay Denmark
Editors:
Gail Showalter, Deborah
Wallach
Assistant Editor:
Randall Coleman
Foley
Artist:
Marko Costanzo
Editors:
Bruce Pross, Frank Kern,
Steven Visscher
**Sound Effects/Foleys
Produced at**
C-5, Inc
Dolby Stereo Consultant
Robert F. Warren
Dialect Consultant
Richard Ericson
**Entomological
Consultants**
John E. Rawlins, PhD,
Sally Love
Police Consultant
Walter 'O. J.' Oggier
Transportation Captain
John Leonidas

**Transportation
Co-Captain**
Dennis Radesky
Craft Services
Richard Fishwick
Stunt Co-ordinator
John Robotham
Stuntmen
Walt Robles, George Wilbur,
Mike Cassidy
Moth Wrangler/Stylist
Raymond A. Mendez
**Assistant Moth
Wrangler/Stylist**
Leanore G. Drogin
Dog Trainer
Christie Miele
Unit Publicist
Judy Arthur

Cast
Jodie Foster
Clarice Starling
Anthony Hopkins
Dr Hannibal Lecter
Scott Glenn
Jack Crawford
Ted Levine
Jame Gumb
Anthony Heald
Dr Frederick Chilton
Brooke Smith
Catherine Martin
Diane Baker
Senator Ruth Martin
Kasi Lemmons
Ardelia Mapp
Charles Napier
Lt Boyle

Tracey Walter
Lamar
Roger Corman
FBI Director Hayden Burke
Ron Vawter
Paul Krendler
Danny Darst
Sgt Tate
Frankie Faison
Barney
Paul Lazar
Pilcher
Dan Butler
Roden
Chris Isaak
SWAT commander
Lawrence A. Bonney
FBI instructor
Lawrence T. Wrentz
Agent Burroughs
Don Brockett
friendly psychopath
Frank Seals Jr
brooding psychopath
Stuart Rudin
Miggs
Masha Skorobogatov
young Clarice
Jeffrie Lane
Clarice's father
Leib Lensky
Mr Lang
Red Schwartz
Mr Lang's driver
Jim Roche
TV evangelist
James B. Howard
boxing instructor

Bill Miller
Mr Brigham
Chuck Aber
Agent Terry
Gene Borkan
Oscar
Pat McNamara
Sheriff Perkins
Kenneth Utt
Dr Akin
'Darla'
'Precious', Jame Gumb's
dog
Adelle Lutz
TV anchor woman
Obba Babatunde
TV anchor man
George Michael
TV sportscaster
Jim Dratfield
Senator Martin's aide
Stanton-Miranda
1st reporter
Rebecca Saxon
2nd reporter
Cynthia Ettinger
Officer Jacobs
Brent Hinkley
Officer Murray
Steve Wyatt
airport flirt
Alex Coleman
Sgt Pembry
David Early
spooked Memphis cop
Andre Blake
tall Memphis cop
Bill Dalzell III
distraught Memphis cop

Daniel von Bargen
SWAT communicator
Tommy LaFitte
SWAT shooter
Josh Broder
EMS attendant
Buzz Kilman
EMS driver
Harry Northup
Mr Bimmel
Lauren Roselli
Stacy Hubka
Lamont Arnold
flower delivery man

[uncredited]
George A. Romero
detective with walkie talkie
in Memphis

[role deleted]
Philip Bosco
Dr Danielsen of Johns
Hopkins

9,518 feet
105 minutes

Dolby SR
Colour by
Technicolor, Inc.
Prints by
DeLuxe
MPAA: 30301

Credits compiled by
Markku Salmi,
BFI Filmographic Unit

Also Published